80 recipes
for your...
Halogen
Oven

80 recipes
for your...
Halogen Oven

Richard Ehrlich

Photography by Will Heap

Kyle Cathie Ltd

For Ruth

First published in Great Britain in 2010 by
Kyle Cathie Limited
23 Howland Street, London W1T 4AY
general.enquiries@kylecathie.com
www.kylecathie.com

10 9 8 7 6 5 4 3 2 1

ISBN 978-1-85626-959-9

Project editor: Jenny Wheatley
Photographer: Will Heap
Designer: Mark Latter/www.bluedragonfly-uk.com
Food stylist: Jane Lawrie
Props stylist: Sue Rowlands
Copy editor: Constance Novis
Editorial assistant: Elanor Clarke
Production: Gemma John

A Cataloguing In Publication record for this title
is available from the British Library.

Printed and bound by Toppan Leefung Printing Ltd in China

contents

introduction

Whether you've bought a halogen oven or are thinking of buying one, a question might be bouncing around in your head like a marble in a tumble dryer: what on earth is this thing?

I can give you a simple answer. It is an oven. It generates heat, and the heat cooks your food. There really isn't that much more to it, and the 'more' can be mastered in around thirty minutes of hands-on experience. Once you've mastered it, I'll bet that you will love it.

Before I go further, let's kill off a common misunderstanding. Halogen ovens are unrelated to microwave ovens. Microwave ovens cook by using very short radio waves to cause molecular movement inside the food. The oven itself produces no heat. Halogen ovens do produce heat, from a circular halogen lamp in the oven lid. The lamp consists of a tungsten filament inside a glass tube which is filled with inert gas. When the power is switched on, the lamp instantly produces intense heat, with bright reddish light as a by-product.

The lid also incorporates a fan. This circulates the air in the oven, distributing heat more efficiently from top to bottom. The heat is highest on top, so food at the bottom cooks more slowly.

The oven's other great advantage is its compact size – around one-quarter the volume of a full-size domestic oven. Compactness means the air in the oven heats up faster, and with so little need for preheating – plus that whirlpool of fanned heat – it typically cooks 20 to 50 per cent faster than a conventional oven. That translates into quicker meals and energy savings, a major attraction from both an economic and an environmental point of view. And the virtues of speedy cooking for busy home cooks need no explanation here.

What is the halogen oven good for? You'd do better asking what it isn't good for. It roasts beautifully – meat, fish, poultry and vegetables. Bread and baked desserts come out perfect in the twinkling of an eye. And as a grill it is incredibly fast.

Who will benefit from owning a halogen oven? Everyone with the counter space to store it. Since I got mine, I have not used my conventional oven once – and I haven't missed it. And I often need to cook for six people. For anyone who lives in a two- or three-person household, the halogen oven should be the oven of choice. If you live alone, or in a studio flat, it's a no-brainer. And if you go camping in a camper van or at campsites where there is mains electricity, the halogen oven should be your companion.

This is a truly remarkable cooking appliance.

hybrid halogen

Officially, the halogen oven is an oven. Unofficially, it can act as a cross between an oven and a grill. Even when the pan support is at a middle level, the uppermost surface of the food may be quite close to the element. So it doesn't cook just through the hot air swirling around the interior but through the direct heat from the lamp, as in a grill.

This can be a problem in some dishes. If the top of the food is too close to the element, it may brown excessively or even burn before the rest of the food is cooked. As a general rule, therefore, dishes that are quite deep and can't be turned are more difficult to cook under halogen.

In other dishes, the grill/oven combination is a wonderful advantage. You'll see it especially in foods of a certain thickness, such as chicken legs or steaks. By the time the top of the meat is well browned and ready for turning, the underside is already partially cooked. This means that the cooking time on the second side is as little as a quarter of the time needed on top. And it allows you to grill/roast items such as a 7.5cm-thick rib of beef in as little as 20 minutes.

the ring of fire

The halogen oven cooks mostly from one direction – the top – and the heating element does not cover the full area of the oven. The heat right under the element gets really fierce, especially if the food in the oven is at grilling level. It's therefore a good idea take the lid off and move things around during cooking if some pieces are under the element and others are closer to the oven wall. Four pieces of chicken, for instance, will need to be moved around halfway through cooking so those under the lamp get moved to the periphery and those on the outside get their turn under highest heat. This is little different from cooking under ordinary grills, which are often hotter in some places than others.

With dishes containing more than one layer of food, the movement is one of tossing. What starts at the bottom must go to the top, and vice versa. You won't need to do it more than four or five times for a dish that cooks for 20 minutes, so the work is not exactly back-breaking.

finding your level

My recipes specify which level of the oven you should use, and these levels are vitally important. The closer your food is to the element, the faster it will cook and the faster it will brown on top. Sometimes you want that rapid browning, but sometimes you don't, so you have to watch your level. I use three terms here:

Bottom of the oven

Your halogen oven should come with a flat roasting rack which sits right on the floor of the oven; this is what I mean by the bottom. The distance from food to lamp is in the general vicinity of 12.5cm. When you need more distance, use the extender ring (see page 10).

Middle of the oven

This is one rung up, and your oven should come with a roasting rack on longer feet, which will get you here (see page 10). The distance between element and food is impossible to state precisely, but it is in the general vicinity of 7.5cm. Middle position is the overall versatility champion in the halogen oven. It gives the ideal combination of roasting and browning, and it is the position I use most.

Top of the oven and grilling position

These make the food and the element get up close and personal – and the results are great. The halogen oven is by far the fastest grill I've ever used. Jane Lawrie, who did the styling for the photographs in this book, calls it 'a sun bed for food'. But the ovens I've used don't mention the grilling dimension and don't provide equipment that enables you to use it. You will have to improvise, and this requires a bit of ingenuity. Just find other cooking dishes or racks that let you put the cooking dish/rack close to the element. For top of the oven, figure on a distance of 5cm from the element. A distance of 2.5cm will be fine for grilling position.

All the recipes here indicate the best cooking level, but you'll have to acquire a certain amount of wisdom on your own. How could it be otherwise, when I don't know which oven and which cooking vessels you will be using? I promise, however, that acquiring wisdom on your own will not take long.

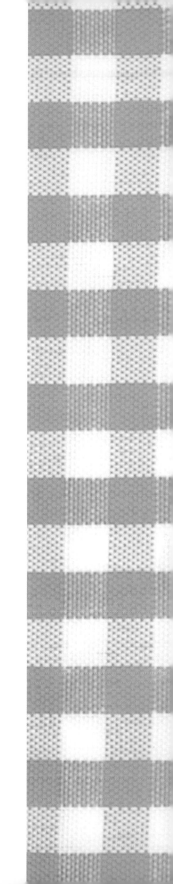

some nuts and bolts

Here are a few essential points about your oven.

where to position it

There are just two vital points. One: the oven should have clear space around it, for the stand (see below) and for freedom from worry about getting the hot element close to anything that might burn or melt. Two: there should be nothing overhead (shelves, for instance) which would make it difficult to lift the lid off.

extra gear

Halogen ovens come with some bits and pieces, either bought separately or as part of the package. They may include:

1. A perforated crisping tray
2. A rack for making toast
3. A flat pan for frying
4. An extender ring
5. A hinged handle for lifting hot dishes
6. A stand to keep the lid on when it isn't in use
7. A roasting rack for bottom position in the oven
8. A roasting rack for middle position in the oven

Items 1 and 2 are strictly optional. I have both, but don't often use them. If you use a crisping tray (for pizza bases and the like), you will want one for your halogen oven as well. Making toast in the halogen oven is possible, and I do it, but it's not the best use of the appliance.

Items 3 to 8 are essential, and you should buy them if they were not included with your oven. The flat pan is useful for many of the dishes here. The extender ring allows you to cook large pieces of meat, and deeper cakes and vegetable dishes, because it gets the food further away from the lamp. The stand: in theory you can put the lid on your work surface, but it's much easier (and safer) to keep it on the stand. And the two racks give you full flexibility as to where in the oven you're going to do your cooking. Apart from all that you just need cooking vessels, many of which you may already have. The most useful and versatile are thin, flat-bottomed metals dishes (15–25cm) for rapid cooking of meat and vegetables, and deeper dishes for stews, sauces and so on.

Important: use only dishes that leave a gap of at least 2.5cm between the dish and the oven wall. This is to facilitate lifting and allow efficient circulation of heat around the oven.

the timer

You need to use the oven timer to switch the oven on, but you don't need to use the oven timer as your alarm. I find it easier to use another timer, because I don't necessarily want the oven to turn off automatically: more cooking time may be needed, and I want to have a timer that keeps going beep-beep-beep so I'm sure to hear it. You will find your own way.

When you lift the lid off to test, turn or inspect your food, the timer will go off automatically. When you put the lid back on and put the handle back down, the oven will turn back on and resume cooking where it left off.

top temperatures

Some halogen ovens I have encountered go only up to 200°C. This is not high enough. If you are buying, make sure that the oven goes up to 250°C or 260°C. I have given both temperatures in the recipes calling for maximum heat. I have also experimented with cooking the same dish at both 250°C and 260°C, and have found no appreciable difference in cooking time. But if you have 260°C on your oven, use it.

above left:
The extender ring in action.

above right:
That clever lifting handle.

a word about safety

The halogen oven incorporates a clever safety mechanism: the power goes off when you lift the handle, which is the only way to take the lid off. As long as you don't touch the metal or glass on the lid while it's really hot, it's quite difficult to burn yourself. But, needless to say, you must avoid letting the handle go down – switching the lamp on – when the lid is not sitting on the oven bowl.

Occasionally the food inside gets very smoky, especially when it is being cooked in grilling position, but it never flames up – probably because there isn't enough air in there. Both bowl and lid can get very hot when you've been cooking something for a long time (anything over 30–40 minutes, which is an eternity in halogen-time). Handle with care and you'll be fine. Note also that the oven stinks up your kitchen less than a conventional oven because it's completely sealed.

the voyeur in the kitchen

Halogen cooking is fun. You can watch the food changing minute by minute and sometimes second by second. This makes the cooking process intimate and exciting. You may find yourself crouched with your nose close to the glass, and this culinary voyeurism becomes dangerously addictive. You have been warned.

Of course, the transparency has practical advantages: when you can see how the food is cooking, you can also see when something is going wrong. And often you don't even need to open the oven door. It's practical, not just fun.

cleaning

Halogen ovens have a cleaning procedure. On mine, you use around 4cm of water and a squirt of washing-up liquid at a low temperature for 10 minutes. I've done it once, and it didn't work that well. I find that washing the bowl in the sink is much more efficient.

Cleaning the lid is trickier, because the element shouldn't get wet. I have had perfectly good results washing down with a soapy brush, then wiping with a wet cloth to eliminate grime and washing-up liquid.

Whatever you do, don't use abrasives on the glass. And do clean your oven regularly. Heavy build-ups of grime are harder to shift.

right:
Watching your dinner cook
can become dangerously
addictive.

a note on the recipes

Most of the recipes in this book use relatively few ingredients. This reflects the way I cook. I prefer to buy good ingredients and flavour them fairly simply. But it's also a matter of practicality. Too many recipes urge home cooks to go and buy a long list of ingredients which may never get used again.

So I take a more relaxed approach to ingredients. If a recipe would be perfect with chervil and 95 per cent perfect with parsley, I will go for parsley every time. Parsley you can use every day. Chervil? If you can even find it, you're probably not going to use the remainder before it yellows, wilts and has to be thrown away.

In short, practicality is the guiding principle here. When you're coming to grips with halogen, you don't need to get too fancy. That can come later, if you wish.

vegetables

When it comes to cooking vegetables in the halogen oven you are spoilt for choice. Anything that's naturally thin and uniform is great – asparagus springs instantly to mind. Certain vegetables, especially those that are very uneven in shape and size, such as broccoli and cauliflower, are not well suited to the halogen oven. However, anything that can be sliced thinly works wonderfully, so courgettes, aubergines, peppers, beetroot and fennel all feature prominently here. The only trick, if you can call it that, is to make sure the vegetables are coated with oil so they don't dry out. One of the great thrills of halogenised vegetables is the way they readily and quickly take on some browning, which makes them taste even better. You can brown them (or even blacken them) in spots or brown them really deeply. Very tasty.

Roasting is one of the best ways of cooking this seasonal delicacy, and the halogen oven speeds things up nicely.

speedy asparagus

serves 2–3 as a side dish

1 large bunch (about 400g) asparagus, ends trimmed off and washed
2 tablespoons extra virgin olive oil
coarse salt

Put the asparagus in a flat dish that will hold them in one or two layers. Drizzle on the oil, then sprinkle on some coarse salt. Cook at the top of the oven at 250°C/260°C for 7–8 minutes until they're done all the way through and well browned on top. You can test for doneness by sticking a sharp knife into a spear; if you want the asparagus crunchier, which is also very good, cook for a few minutes extra.

Roasting enhances the sweet, delicate flavour of a fresh, aromatic bulb of fennel. Don't be tempted to cut out the woody core; it helps hold the pieces together during cooking.

fast fresh fennel

serves 4 as a side dish

2 fat fennel bulbs, trimmed and quartered
vegetable oil
salt and freshly ground black pepper
1 tablespoon extra virgin olive oil
1 teaspoon balsamic vinegar
juice of ½ small lemon or ¼ large lemon

Rub the fennel quarters all over with just enough vegetable oil to coat them thoroughly. (You shouldn't need much more than 1 tablespoon.) Season with salt and freshly ground black pepper, and cook at 250°C/260°C at the middle of the oven until they're done the way you like them: about 10 minutes for al dente; 15 for à point; 20 for soft. Don't worry if the bulbs blacken in spots – this adds complexity to the flavour.

While they're cooking, make a vinaigrette from the remaining ingredients. Pour this over the cooked fennel, which may be served hot or at room temperature.

If you feel it is wasteful to fire up your conventional oven to roast vegetables just for yourself, here is your chance to indulge. One aubergine will feed one person as a side dish, and you can cook up to two at a time. If serving more people, cook in batches.

roasted aubergine

serves 1 as a side dish

1 small aubergine, about 12cm long
2 teaspoons extra virgin olive oil
salt and freshly ground black pepper

Halve the aubergine lengthwise and brush the cut surfaces with the oil. Season with salt and freshly ground black pepper. Place in the oven, cut-side up, and cook at the top at 200°C for 10 minutes. Then turn the aubergine halves over and cook for another 3–5 minutes.

This is incredibly quick and really tasty. The fresh mint – tossed in right at the end with the vinaigrette – adds a lively top note.

peppers and aubergines

**serves 3 as a
side dish**

2 big red peppers, or
  1 red and 1 yellow,
  deseeded and thickly
  sliced
1 medium aubergine,
  thickly sliced
1 tablespoon
  vegetable oil
1 medium onion,
  thickly sliced
1 plump garlic clove,
  finely chopped
1 tablespoon extra
  virgin olive oil
2 teaspoons red wine
  vinegar
4–5 sprigs of fresh
  mint, coarsely
  chopped or torn

Toss the peppers, aubergine and vegetable oil in a large, flat-bottomed dish. Cook at 200°C at the middle of the oven, stirring a few times, until the aubergine is nearly done, about 10 minutes. Add the onion and garlic and continue cooking until the onion is lightly coloured and soft but retaining a good hint of al dente bite, about 5 minutes. Toss with the olive oil, vinegar and mint. Serve either hot or at room temperature.

roasting peppers

The halogen oven is the best tool I've seen for roasting peppers, whether for peeling and slicing or for stuffing (as in the recipe on page 97). The best way to do it is by halving and deseeding, then cooking right under the element (grilling position) for about ten minutes. Only two pepper halves can squeeze in right under the element at a time, but if you put another pepper in the cooking dish (or even two), they will start cooking while the principal peppers are getting blasted by heat. Once the first two halves are done, move the others under the element and they will cook faster.

Wonderful summery flavours from three main ingredients.
The courgettes can be sliced into discs or strips as long
as the pieces are fairly thin.

courgettes, tomatoes and basil

serves 2–4
as a side dish

3 or 4 smallish
   courgettes, thinly
   sliced
small handful of fresh
   basil, leaves only,
   coarsely chopped
   or torn
1 large ripe, red tomato,
   cut into slices about
   1cm thick
extra virgin olive oil
salt and freshly ground
   black pepper

Put half the courgette slices in a thin metal dish about
25cm in diameter. Scatter half the basil over them, then
put the remaining courgettes on top. Cover with the
tomato slices and season with a little salt and plenty of
freshly ground black pepper. Drizzle lightly with oil.

Cook at 250°C/260°C at the middle of the oven until
the top is nicely coloured and the vegetables cooked
the way you like them. To keep a good hint of al dente
firmness, 8–10 minutes should be long enough. For a
softer result, cook for a couple of minutes more. Garnish
with more basil if you wish.

courgettes

Courgettes are one of the best vegetables for cooking in the
halogen oven, and several recipes here feature them in different
guises. They're just as good in very simple presentations,
however. Here are a few of my favourites:

- Halve or quarter the courgettes lengthwise, brush with oil, and
  cook for 7–8 minutes at 250°C/260°C at the middle of the oven.
- Cut into batons about 1cm thick and 7.5cm long, toss with
  oil and cook at 250°C/260°C in the grilling position for about
  5 minutes.
- Grate on a coarse grater and squeeze out as much water as
  possible in a clean tea-towel. Mix with 2 teaspoons of extra
  virgin olive oil per courgette plus salt and black pepper. Put in
  a thin non-stick metal dish, forming a neat, flat disc no more
  than 2.5cm deep. Cook in the grilling position until the top
  is well browned, about 10 minutes. Grated Parmesan can be
  sprinkled on top for the last few minutes of cooking.

This is best using the courgettes and aubergines in their miniature form, available in many Asian and Middle Eastern shops. They are usually about 15cm long. If you can't get them, use the smallest vegetables you can find (especially the aubergines) and cut into pieces about 5cm thick and 15cm long.

courgettes and aubergines:
the chinesey version

serves 3–4

4 small courgettes, halved lengthwise
4 small aubergines, halved lengthwise
1 medium onion, thickly sliced
2 plump garlic cloves, finely chopped
2 thick slices of fresh ginger, peeled and finely chopped
2 tablespoons vegetable oil
salt and freshly ground black pepper
1 tablespoon soy sauce
2 teaspoons red wine vinegar
1 teaspoon sesame oil
coriander leaves, to garnish

Put the vegetables, garlic, ginger and vegetable oil in a flat ovenproof dish that will hold them in a layer no more than 5cm deep. Season with a little salt and plenty of freshly ground black pepper, and toss thoroughly. (You may find it easier to do the tossing in a bowl and then transfer the stuff to the cooking dish.)

Cook at 200°C at the middle of the oven, stirring and tossing every 5 minutes or so, until the vegetables are done the way you like them. I reached perfection – which for me means well coloured and fully soft – after 25 minutes. You may want them cooked more or less than that.

When they're ready, toss them with the soy sauce, red wine vinegar and sesame oil. Garnish with coriander. Serve hot or at room temperature.

Closer to ratatouille, but not identical. Use miniature vegetables if possible but see note on the previous page for choosing the vegetables.

courgettes and aubergines:
the classic version

serves 3–4

4 small courgettes, halved lengthwise
4 small aubergines, halved lengthwise
1 medium onion, thickly sliced
2 plump garlic cloves, finely chopped
60ml passata
2–3 tablespoons extra virgin olive oil
salt and freshly ground black pepper
10–12 cherry tomatoes
basil leaves, to garnish

Put the courgettes, aubergines, onion, garlic, passata and 1 tablespoon of olive oil in a flat ovenproof dish that will hold everything in a layer no more than 5cm deep. Season with a little salt and plenty of freshly ground black pepper, and toss thoroughly. (You may find it easier to do the tossing in a bowl and then transfer the stuff to the cooking dish.)

Cook at 250°C/260°C at the middle of the oven, stirring and tossing every 5 minutes or so, until the vegetables are done the way you like them. This should take about 20 minutes. Add the cherry tomatoes around halfway through the cooking time, so they cook through without turning into complete mush.

When they're ready, toss with more oil (you decide how much) and garnish with basil leaves. Serve hot or at room temperature.

With minimal effort you can make a lovely side dish or garnish in just a few minutes. And with a few minutes more, you can make something substantial enough to serve as a quick pasta sauce.

roasted cherry tomatoes

serves 4 as a side dish, or 2 as a sauce

1 plump garlic clove, finely chopped
1 shallot or 2 spring onions, finely chopped
hefty knob of butter
salt and freshly ground black pepper
400g cherry tomatoes, halved or whole
½ teaspoon dried oregano or dried mixed herbs, such as herbes de Provence
½ teaspoon balsamic vinegar
few drops of lemon juice
8–10 chives, finely chopped

Put the garlic, shallot or spring onions and butter in a flat-bottomed dish at least 25cm in diameter. Season with salt and freshly ground black pepper. Add the tomatoes and herbs, and cook at 200°C at the top of the oven for 1 minute to get the butter melting. Stir well and cook at 250°C/260°C, stirring once, just long enough to heat the tomatoes through and soften them without making them collapse, about 4 minutes. Toss with the acidic ingredients, sprinkle with chives and serve immediately.

To make this into a sauce

Slice 150g of closed-cap mushrooms. Proceed as above, but cook the tomatoes initially for just 2 minutes. Stir in the mushrooms and cook, stirring once or twice, until the mushrooms are just soft enough to eat, about 4–5 minutes. Use finely chopped parsley as a garnish instead of chives, and serve on long pasta, such as spaghetti or linguine.

Note: if you want to serve this at room temperature, use extra virgin olive oil instead of butter. Use 1 tablespoon for the cooking, then add another tablespoon with the acidic stuff.

Life is full of mysteries. Take the halogen oven, for example. It should not excel at cooking tomato sauce, but it does. I suspect the excellence stems from the browning effect of the high over-head heat, which gives the sauce a subtly smoky note. Whatever the explanation, everyone loves this sauce. And it cooks very quickly, which contradicts the received wisdom that tomato sauce has to simmer delicately for centuries. The quantities here make a lot – more than you will need for most dishes – so freeze any that is left over.

an excellent tomato sauce

serves 8–10

1 small onion, finely chopped
1 tablespoon vegetable oil
salt and freshly ground black pepper
2–3 plump garlic cloves, finely chopped
4 x 400g tins chopped tomatoes
2 tablespoons tomato purée
1 tablespoon dried herbs, such as herbes de Provence
1 bay leaf
120–150ml extra virgin olive oil

Put the onion and vegetable oil in a large, flat, fairly deep dish; a 28cm quiche dish is what I used and it was perfect. Season with salt and freshly ground black pepper. Toss well to coat the onions with oil. Cook at 250°C at the top of the oven for 2–3 minutes, just long enough to get the onion sizzling a little and smelling nice. Add the garlic, stir well, and cook for another minute or so to get the garlic very fragrant.

Add the tomatoes, tomato purée, dried herbs and bay leaf, and stir well. Continue cooking, with regular stirring (every 5 minutes or so), until the tomatoes are thickened to the consistency you like, about 20–25 minutes. Touches of deep browning are part of the charm of the sauce, but don't let any pieces of tomato get too black.

The sauce is completed by adding as much extra virgin olive oil as you want. If you are freezing some of the sauce, don't put in the olive oil until you're ready to use it.

This idea came from my brother Henry, and it's one my favourite vegetable dishes for the halogen oven. You can eat it hot or cold, but I think it is best served warm.

warm coleslaw

serves 4–6

1 small onion, coarsely chopped
½ teaspoon each whole cumin, coriander, fenugreek and fennel seeds
2 tablespoons vegetable oil
salt and freshly ground black pepper
1 small white cabbage, cored and thinly sliced
2 small carrots, peeled and coarsely grated
1–1½ tablespoons red wine or cider vinegar

Put the onion, spices and oil in a large, flat, fairly deep dish; I used a 28cm quiche dish, which was perfect. Season with salt and freshly ground black pepper, toss well to coat the onions with oil, and cook at 250°C/260°C at the middle of the oven for 2–3 minutes, just long enough to lightly toast the spices and get the onion smelling nice.

Add the cabbage and carrots. Toss really well to coat them with oil, then return to the oven and continue cooking until the vegetables are very hot and slightly softened but retain a good al dente crunch, about 15–20 minutes, depending on how much crunch you want. Toss during cooking at least 4 or 5 times so all the vegetables get some close exposure to the element's heat. There will be lightly blackened bits here and there, which adds complexity to the flavour. When the dish is cooked, toss with the vinegar. Serve immediately or leave to cool for 20–30 minutes before serving.

I love cooked carrots, especially when they take on a good suntan from long exposure to high heat. These take only 20 minutes.

simplest carrots ever

serves 6 or more

6 large carrots, cut into chunks about 2.5cm thick
1–2 tablespoons vegetable oil
salt and freshly ground black pepper

Put the carrots in an ovenproof dish at least 7.5cm deep. Toss with enough oil to coat the pieces lightly but thoroughly, and season. Cook at 250°C/260°C at the middle of the oven, stirring and tossing every 5 minutes or so, until the carrots are cooked the way you like them.

Three favourite carrot seasonings
• Fresh ginger and garlic, finely chopped
• 1 big shallot, finely chopped
• A dainty dollop of orange marmalade during cooking and lemon juice before serving

The ultra-simple approach of this recipe preserves the fantastic flavour of this undeservedly underrated vegetable in its pure form. You can use this as a side dish on its own or as a component in an assembled salad, co-starring goat's cheese and some mixed leaves, perhaps with a few toasted pine nuts sprinkled on.

roasted beetroot

serves 4

4 small or 2 medium beetroot, vigorously scrubbed until not a single bit of grit remains
vegetable oil
salt and freshly ground black pepper
1 tablespoon red wine vinegar

Trim the ends of the beetroot and halve (if small) or quarter (if larger); do not peel. Put them in a flat-bottomed dish and brush or rub all over with the oil, then season with salt (but no pepper yet). Cook at 200°C at the top of the oven, until they're just tender, about 20 minutes. Season with freshly ground black pepper and serve hot or at room temperature with the vinegar sprinkled over them. Or leave them undressed in anticipation of salad dressing.

The dry-fried beans of Chinese cuisine are one of the world's great vegetable dishes, and you can achieve something similar in a halogen oven. The only tricks are to make sure the beans are well coated with oil and to toss them a few times during cooking.

blackened french beans

serves 4 as a side dish

250g beans, topped and tailed
1–2 tablespoons vegetable oil
freshly ground black pepper
1 shallot, finely chopped
1 plump garlic clove, finely chopped
2 teaspoons soy sauce
few drops of sesame oil
1 teaspoon sesame seeds (optional)

Put the beans in a large flat-bottomed dish and toss very well with the vegetable oil and some freshly ground black pepper. Cook at 200°C at the top of the oven, stirring 3 or 4 times, until they're just soft enough to eat, about 10 minutes. When they seem to be nearly done, toss with the shallot and garlic and cook for a couple of minutes more. To serve, toss with the soy sauce and sesame oil. You could also sprinkle on some sesame seeds, dry-fried in a small pan until lightly browned.

You will be tempted to save this dish for yourself
and your nearest and dearest – it is utterly delicious.
It's essential to use fairly small aubergines for this.
Larger ones would be tough

stuffed aubergines

serves 2

2 smallish aubergines,
    about 15cm long
1 tablespoon vegetable oil
2 hefty slices red or
    yellow onion, coarsely
    chopped
1 plump garlic clove,
    finely chopped
2 small tomatoes
large pinch of dried
    oregano
large handful of parsley,
    finely chopped
small handful of dried
    breadcrumbs (optional)
salt and freshly ground
    black pepper
4–6 tablespoons coarsely
    chopped or grated
    hard, sharp cheese
    (e.g. mature Cheddar
    or Gruyère) – optional

Halve the aubergines lengthwise without topping or tailing
(this helps them keep their shape and retain the stuffing
rather than spilling it into the cooking dish). Using a small,
sharp knife in tandem with a teaspoon, remove as much of
the flesh as possible. This will probably mean leaving the
shell with about 1cm of flesh attached to it, which happens
to be exactly what you're aiming for.

Put the aubergine shells on a thin flat metal dish and lightly
brush or wipe the insides with vegetable oil. Cook at the
middle of the oven for 5–10 minutes at 250°C/260°C.
This should give you just enough time to prepare the
stuffing. Finely chop the aubergine flesh and mix with all the
ingredients except the cheese, and season well with salt
and freshly ground black pepper.

When the aubergine shells are fairly soft, carefully spoon
the stuffing into them. Cook at 200°C at the middle of the
oven until the aubergines are very nearly cooked (taste a
fragment to test); this should take about 20 minutes. At this
point, sprinkle the cheese over them (if using) and cook until
the aubergines are completely softened (or just continue
cooking without the cheese). Either way, it will take another
5 minutes or so.

This is a classic French concoction of chopped mushrooms cooked to dryness with butter and shallots or spring onions. It is incredibly versatile. You can use it as a topping for fish or meat, a filling for jacket potatoes, a sauce for vegetables or just a great canapé – and much more besides. The quantities here make about 350g of duxelles. This is a lot, but you can freeze the surplus and keep it on hand for jazzing up everyday meals.

duxelles

serving numbers depend on how you use them

2 shallots or spring onions, finely chopped
1 teaspoon dried mixed herbs, such as herbes de Provence
500g white or brown closed-cap mushrooms, finely chopped
75ml single or double cream
salt and freshly ground black pepper
2 large knobs butter (about 50g)
large handful of flat-leaf parsley, finely chopped

Put all the ingredients except the butter and parsley in a large, deep, flat dish. Season well with salt and freshly ground black pepper and dot with the butter. Cook at 200°C at the middle of the oven, stirring well once the butter has melted and then stirring frequently (every few minutes is good) throughout. The mushrooms should end up being very dry and the volume reduced by up to 80 per cent. This should take about 20 minutes but it could take as many as 30. Stir in the parsley, cook for another minute and turn off the heat.

For canapés

Toast slices of white bread, then put the duxelles mixture on top and cook at the middle of the oven at 200°C until bubbling hot (about 5–10 minutes); or cook them in the conventional oven if the oven is on anyway. For a nicer presentation, the bread can be pressed into small muffin tins to form a cup. Toast these in a hot oven, then fill with duxelles and bake until bubbling.

mushrooms

Mushrooms of all shapes and sizes are very well suited to the halogen oven. They love its speed and its intense heat, and the oven loves them back because their compact size, whether whole or in pieces, lends itself to easy cooking. On page 35 you will find two more of my favourite fungal feasts, halogen-style.

You can vary the flavourings of roast mushrooms endlessly, but the key to success lies in not overcooking them. It's a good idea to cook them when you are using the oven for something else.

roasted mushrooms

serves 2 as a light lunch or 4 as a side dish

250g closed-cap chestnut mushrooms
2 tablespoons extra virgin olive oil
2 plump garlic cloves
5–6 sprigs of fresh thyme

Mix all the ingredients thoroughly. There should be enough oil to coat the mushrooms well, but they don't have to be soaked through. Put everything in a flat-bottomed non-stick dish and cook at the top of the oven at 200°C, stirring a few times. They should be finished in 5–6 minutes.

Here is a quick but satisfying weekend lunch (served on toast) or a topping for jacket potatoes or pasta. Be sure to use high-quality dry-cured British bacon or Italian pancetta.

mushrooms, peas & bacon

serves 2–3 as a main course or 4 as a side dish

100g thick-sliced bacon or pancetta, rinds removed and cut into 1cm lardons
250g frozen peas
300g small button mushrooms, cleaned well and stalk ends trimmed
freshly ground black pepper
1 large garlic clove, finely chopped
large handful of parsley, finely chopped

Put the lardons in a flat non-stick dish and cook near the top of the oven at 250°C/260°C, stirring a few times, until they are well browned, about 4–5 minutes. When they are done, spoon out all but 2 tablespoons or so of fat from the dish.

While the bacon is in the oven, cook the peas until barely done either in the microwave or in a small covered saucepan; cook until they are about 1 minute short of ready. If they are done before the bacon, drain off excess water and leave to cool. Place the mushrooms in the dish with the bacon and grind on a generous dose of black pepper. Stir well to coat thoroughly with fat. Turn the heat up and cook at 200°C, stirring a few times, until the mushrooms are nearly done, about 5 minutes. Stir in the garlic, then add the peas. Cook at 200°C until the peas and bacon are heated through, about 2–3 minutes. Sprinkle with the parsley and serve immediately, straight from the dish.

eggs

Eggs present something of a challenge to halogen cooks, but it is in no way insurmountable. The overhead heat can cause problems for baked egg dishes if the surface turns too deeply brown before the eggs on the bottom set fully. After a bit of experimentation, however, I discovered a couple of simple solutions to this and have come up with any number of good dishes. I hope you enjoy them.

tortillas and frittatas

It took me a while to figure out how to
solve a basic problem with these versatile,
flexible creatures: getting the egg on the
bottom to cook fully while not overcooking
the surface. In the event, the solution
proved simplicity itself. All you need to
do is make sure the pan is hot when you
put the eggs in.

When asparagus is in season and you are looking for ever more ways to enjoy them, this makes a great lunch dish.

asparagus and onion frittata

serves 2–3

8–10 fairly thin spears of asparagus, ends trimmed
1 tablespoon vegetable oil
salt and freshly ground black pepper
3–4 thin slices of red onion
3 free-range eggs
1 tablespoon extra virgin olive oil

Cut the asparagus in half and put them in a small, flat-bottomed metal dish, about 15cm in diameter. Toss well with the vegetable oil and season with a good dose of salt and freshly ground black pepper. Cook at 200°C at the top of the oven, stirring a few times, until the asparagus is very nearly cooked, about 5 minutes. Add the onion slices and stir them in well. Cook for a few minutes more. In the meantime, beat the eggs with the olive oil.

Add the eggs to the dish, tilting it if necessary to spread the egg out evenly. Continue cooking until the eggs are just cooked through, about 3–4 minutes. Serve hot or at room temperature.

Using a halogen oven, all it takes is twenty minutes to cook this classic Spanish tortilla.

spanish tortilla

serves 2

1 small potato, chopped into small chunks
1 tablespoon vegetable oil
salt and freshly ground black pepper
½ small onion, roughly chopped
2 free-range eggs
a few sprigs of parsley, finely chopped
2 teaspoons extra virgin olive oil

Put the potato into a small, flat-bottomed metal dish, about 15cm in diameter. Mix well with the oil and a good dose of salt and pepper. Cook at 200°C at the top of the oven, stirring a few times, until the potato is very nearly cooked, about 10 minutes. Add the onion, stir in well and cook for a few minutes more. In the meantime, beat the eggs with the parsley and olive oil.

Add the eggs to the dish, tilting it if necessary to spread them out evenly. Continue cooking until the eggs are just cooked through, about 3–4 minutes. Serve hot or at room temperature.

Don't take title of this recipe too seriously. It's just a play on the name of the great Roman dish that features all these ingredients – minus the pasta.

eggs à la carbonara

serves 2–3

75–100g pancetta or
   top-quality streaky
   bacon, cut into lardons
   about 1cm thick
1 medium onion, coarsely
   chopped
salt and freshly ground
   black pepper
3–4 free-range eggs,
   beaten
small handful of freshly
   grated Parmesan
small handful flat-leaf
   parsley, chopped

Cook the lardons in a flat, non-stick dish at middle level until they're just turning brown. Add the onion, toss well and season with a little salt and plenty of freshly ground black pepper. Continue cooking for 4 or 5 minutes, until the onion is blackening in places, turning brown in others, softening somewhat and smelling really great. In the meantime, mix the eggs with the cheese and parsley.

Remove the dish from the oven and position the cooking rack at grilling level. Carefully pour the eggs onto the lardons and onion, trying not to splosh any over the sides of the dish. Put the dish back in the oven and continue cooking until the eggs are well browned on top and barely cooked underneath. This can take anything from 4 to 6 minutes, and you can check them by sliding a spatula or palette knife underneath and lifting the eggs up; they should be nearly set, with very little liquid. Slide the eggs onto a large serving plate and serve immediately with toast.

This rich and filling dish will serve six people but be warned: if you eat it more than twice a month, don't tell your cardiologist. Cooking this dish in two steps overcomes the problem of cooking a deep layer of egg right through.

baked eggs with bacon, cheese and onion

serves 6

5–6 thick slices of bacon or pancetta, weighing about 100g, cut into thick slices
1 large onion, coarsely chopped
salt and freshly ground black pepper
large knob of butter
6 free-range eggs
50ml single cream (optional)
100g sharp Cheddar, freshly grated

Put the bacon (or pancetta) in a heavy, flat-bottomed dish of about 20cm in diameter. Cook at 200°C at the middle of the oven until the bacon is lightly browned and is rendering up some of its fat. Add the onion and butter, season with a little salt and a lot of freshly ground black pepper, and cook until the onion is slightly softened and lightly coloured.

In the meantime, beat 3 of the eggs with half the cream (if using) and half the cheese. Add to the dish and stir well, then continue cooking until the eggs are looking fairly well set, about 5–10 minutes. In the meantime, beat the other 3 eggs with the remaining cream and cheese. Add to the pan and continue cooking until the dish is set all the way through, with just a little bit of liquid at the bottom, about another 5–10 minutes. You can check them by sliding a spatula or palette knife underneath and lifting the eggs up; they should be nearly set, with very little liquid. Leave to rest for a few minutes and serve hot, with toast or a potato salad.

Weekend lunch terrain. You can use chorizo, louganika, merguez, or any other spicy sausage of that type that takes your fancy.

spicy sausage and eggs

serves 2–3

110g spicy sausage
4 free-range eggs, beaten

Cut the sausage on the bias into 5mm slices. Put the slices into a large, thin, flat-bottomed metal dish, such as a pie dish. Place at the top of the oven and cook at 250°C/260°C until the sausage is lightly browned and sizzling energetically, about 3–5 minutes. If there is a lot of oil in the dish, spoon out all but about 1 tablespoon. Add the beaten eggs and swirl the dish around to get even coating on the bottom of the dish. Return to the oven and continue cooking until the eggs are just set, about 5–8 minutes. Serve immediately with pitta bread (try the recipe on page 118) and a green salad.

variation

You can also a less spicy, more home-style-comfort-food version of this using good sausages from a traditional butcher. They should not be too fine in texture, but apart from the flavour's up to you. Remove the skins from the sausages and crumble them roughly. Add a little vegetable oil to the cooking dish, then proceed as described above. Plan for a few minutes of extra cooking time, however, because the sausages have to cook from raw. And note: black pudding could be used in the same way as long as it is not too fatty.

fish

When I started out with the halogen oven, I feared it would be suitable only for thinnish fillets and small shellfish. I shouldn't have worried. As it turned out, with minimal tweaks, plenty of traditional fish dishes can be adapted for halogen, even stews and whole roast fish of considerable size. The halogenic ability to brown and bake at the same time is especially nice, giving some remarkable complexity of flavour even in very simple dishes. Having said all that, I must add that simple fish dishes, quickly cooked, will be the category that appeals to many people. Midweek dinners were never so speedy.

This began life as a pasta sauce for my daughter Ruth, who loved it, but it could also be served on its own. If that's what you choose to do, use just half the extra virgin olive oil at the end. Midweek cooks, take note: two of the principal ingredients come from the freezer, and preparing the sauce takes little more time than it does to boil water for pasta. You can even defrost the prawns and peas in the fridge before leaving for work.

prawn, pepper and pea pasta sauce

serves 2, or 2–3 as a pasta sauce

1 medium yellow pepper, chopped into small dice
1 or 2 spring onions or 1 large shallot, finely chopped
small red chilli, deseeded if you wish and finely chopped (optional)
1 tablespoon vegetable oil
salt and freshly ground black pepper
1 plump garlic clove, finely chopped
180g frozen peeled prawns, defrosted
125g frozen peas, defrosted
2 tablespoons extra virgin olive oil

Mix the pepper, spring onions or shallot and chilli (if using) with the vegetable oil in a large, flat dish. Season with salt and freshly ground black pepper. Cook at 250°C/260°C at the middle of the oven just long enough to soften the pepper slightly (about 10 minutes). Stir in the garlic and prawns and continue cooking until the prawns are barely cooked, about 5 minutes. Add the peas for the final 2 minutes of cooking, just long enough to get them good and hot. You will need to stir it a couple of times. Stir in the olive oil just before serving.

This makes an absurdly impressive starter for a dinner party. If you can't get closed-cap button mushrooms of the right size, use six large open-cap mushrooms with two scallops, halved, in each one. To serve these in a really fancy manner, present them on toasted rounds of white bread or surround them with a little rocket dressed in good extra virgin olive oil.

mushrooms with a scallop stuffing

serves 4 as a starter

1 lemon
12 large closed-cap
  button mushrooms,
  each 5–7.5cm in
  diameter
8–10 sprigs of parsley,
  finely chopped
1 large shallot, finely
  chopped
12 good-sized dots of
  butter, each about
  the size of a big pea
12 large scallops,
  whites only, washed
  and trimmed
50g butter, melted
paprika or Spanish
  pimentón
salt and freshly ground
  black pepper

Cut a wedge off the lemon. Using a small, sharp knife, remove 8 small pieces – without pith, seeds or segment walls – about the size of your thumbnail. Set aside.

Remove the stalks from the mushrooms and save for another recipe (or just eat them). Place the mushrooms on a metal dish that will hold them in a single layer. Sprinkle a little parsley in the cup of each mushroom, then follow it with some chopped shallot, a piece of lemon and a dot of butter. Now put in the scallops, pushing them down firmly. (This recipe may be prepared in advance up to this point and refrigerated.)

Brush melted butter liberally onto each scallop, and all the exposed surfaces of the mushrooms. Dust each scallop very lightly with paprika or pimentón and season with a little salt and plenty of freshly ground black pepper. Cluster the stuffed mushrooms towards the centre of the dish.

Cook at 250°C/260°C at the top of the oven, in grilling position, until the scallops are lightly browned on top and the mushrooms are bubbling. This could take as little as 5 minutes and should not take more than 7.

This is another dish that can be eaten solo or used as a pasta sauce.
The quantity will serve two on its own (deploy crusty bread to soak
up the heavenly tomato sauce) or three as a sauce for pasta.

clams with tomato sauce

serves 2–3

¼ recipe for tomato sauce
    (see page 25)
pinch of paprika or
    Spanish pimentón
300g small clams
2 tablespoons extra
    virgin olive oil
small handful of parsley,
    finely chopped

Put the sauce in an ovenproof dish with the paprika or pimentón. Cook for a few minutes in the middle of the oven at 250°C/260°C, just long enough to get it good and hot. Add the clams, stir well, and continue cooking – with regular stirring – until they have opened all the way, about 6–8 minutes. Stir in the oil and parsley, and serve as you wish. The sauce can be left to cool its heels for a little while if it's done before the pasta is cooked.

This is inspired by a dim sum dish using baby octopus
that I ate in Yum Cha, a Chinese restaurant in London.

squid with worcestershire sauce

serves 2

500g cleaned squid,
    sliced into bite-sized
    pieces
2 teaspoons honey
1 tablespoon vegetable oil
2 teaspoons
    Worcestershire sauce
1 tablespoon soy sauce
pinch of Chinese
    five-spice powder

Toss all the ingredients thoroughly and refrigerate, if possible, for 1–2 hours. Place in a flat-bottomed dish and cook at 250°C/260°C, in grilling position, until the squid is just cooked and lightly coloured, about 7–8 minutes. Toss the squid a few times during cooking and serve straight from the dish so the delectable pan juices can be eaten with it.

Serve on a bed of rice or Chinese noodles tossed with sliced spring onions, finely chopped fresh ginger and sesame oil.

This delicious dish would be a big hit at a small dinner party. It's so easy and quick, though, you could really cook it for an ordinary midweek supper. If you happen to have cooked rice on hand, that makes a fine alternative to the breadcrumbs.

stuffed squid

serves 4

4 medium-sized squid,
   weighing about
   175g apiece
1 small garlic clove,
   finely chopped
large handful of parsley,
   coarsely chopped
large handful of dried
   breadcrumbs
8 cherry tomatoes, halved
½ teaspoon grated
   or finely chopped
   lemon zest
juice of ½ lemon
1 tablespoon dry white
   wine
vegetable oil

Clean the squid if they have not already been cleaned. Chop the tentacles and mix them with all the remaining ingredients. Stuff the mixture into the squid sacs and then place them in a lightly oiled, flat-bottomed dish. Lightly brush with vegetable oil. Cook at 200°C at the middle of the oven until the squid is just done but lightly browned on top, and the stuffing is piping hot all the way through, about 10–12 minutes. This can be served with rice or just some good crusty bread.

This very easy dish, ready in little more than ten minutes once all the ingredients have been prepared, makes a great summertime lunch. For the best flavour, take it out of the fridge to rest for 30 minutes or so before serving.

seafood salad

serves 3–4

1 large red pepper, deseeded and cut into thickish pieces, then each piece halved crosswise
1 tablespoon vegetable oil
salt and freshly ground black pepper
300g cleaned squid, cut into bite-sized pieces
250g raw prawns, peeled
2 celery stalks, cut on the bias into thin slices
1 small chilli, deseeded if you wish and finely chopped (optional)
1 plump garlic clove, finely chopped
1 tablespoon extra virgin olive oil
juice of ½ lemon
small handful of parsley or coriander, chopped

Mix the pepper and vegetable oil in a large, flat dish (a quiche dish about 28cm in diameter is perfect) and season with salt and freshly ground black pepper. Cook near the top of the oven at 250°C/260°C for a couple of minutes, then stir in the squid, prawns, celery, chilli (if using) and garlic. Cook, stirring several times, until the squid and prawns are just done, about 8–10 minutes. Leave to cool, then stir in the olive oil, lemon juice and parsley or coriander. Serve with pitta bread (see page 118) or just some good crusty bread.

These kebabs can be made with any firm-fleshed white fish as long as it's thick enough to cut into pieces roughly 2.5cm square. Or, if the expense doesn't frighten you, treat yourself to some big scallops.

fish and bacon kebabs

serves 2 as a main course or 4 as a starter

8 chunks of white fish, roughly 2.5cm square, or 8 big scallops
small handful of parsley, finely chopped
large pinch of paprika or Spanish pimentón
freshly ground black pepper
4 or 8 very thin slices of good dry-cured bacon, rinds removed

Check there are no large bones in the fish. Mix the parsley and paprika or pimentón and add a good grinding of pepper. Roll the fish pieces in this mixture. Roll a slice of bacon around each piece and secure on a short metal skewer. (The pieces can also be cooked without skewers as long as the seam side is facing down in the dish.) The kebabs can be prepared in advance to this point, then stored in the fridge covered in clingfilm.

When you are ready to cook, place the pieces in a flat metal dish and cook at 250°C/260°C in grilling position until the top of the bacon is nicely browned and the fish is just cooked, about 5–6 minutes. Serve on a bed of rice or buttered noodles.

Note: the bacon must be dry-cured or it will throw off liquid that impairs the quality of the dish.

Skate, with its meaty texture and relatively flat, even surface, takes very well to the halogen oven. The two sauces here are skate classics.

two ways with skate

mustard and cream

serves 4

2 large or 4 small skate wings, weighing about 450g or 250g apiece
100ml single cream
50ml Dijon mustard
salt and freshly ground black pepper
50ml dry white wine
small handful of parsley, finely chopped, to garnish

Halve the wings if they are large and put them in a heavy, flat-bottomed dish. Mix the cream and mustard with a lot of salt and freshly ground black pepper, then pour over the fish. Pour the wine into the dish (not onto the fish itself) and cook at 200°C at the top of the oven. Spoon the liquid over the fish once or twice, until the fish is lightly browned on top and just cooked through, about 15 minutes. Garnish with parsley and serve with plain rice or simply cooked potatoes.

capers and lemon

serves 4

2 large or 4 small skate wings, weighing about 450g or 250g apiece
2 tablespoons capers, coarsely chopped
4 thin slices of lemon
salt and freshly ground black pepper
4 small knobs of butter
50ml dry white wine
small handful of parsley, finely chopped, to garnish

Halve the wings if they are large. Put half the capers and the lemon slices in a heavy, flat-bottomed dish and set the skate on top. Season with a bit of salt and lots of freshly ground black pepper. Put the remaining capers and the knobs of butter on top of the fish. Pour the wine into the dish (not onto the fish itself) and cook at 200°C at the top of the oven. Spoon the liquid over the fish once or twice, and continue to cook until the fish is lightly browned on top and just cooked through, about 15 minutes. Garnish with parsley and serve with plain rice or simply cooked potatoes.

The name refers not to a narrow-minded fish but to a good way of cooking the stuff. It originates, I think, in France, where it's called *'d'un côté'* (cooked on one side only). The method suits salmon particularly well because salmon's skin goes crunchy under dry heat, and some people love that crunch. Other people never touch fish skin, however delectable it may be, but the method has something to offer them too. As it's the method that matters here, I've given only a per-person procedure, but you can cook salmon this way for a maximum of four.

one-sided salmon

crunchy skin

serves 1

vegetable oil
1 salmon fillet, preferably
  from the middle,
  weighing about 125g
salt and freshly ground
  black pepper
lemon or lime wedges,
  to serve

Lightly brush or wipe a flat, non-stick dish with vegetable oil and put in the salmon skin-side up. Brush very lightly with vegetable oil and season with salt and freshly ground black pepper. Cook at 250°C/260°C in the middle of the oven for 7–8 minutes, until the skin is brown and crunchy. Lift one corner to see if it's cooked the way you like it on the flesh side, then continue with the cooking for another 1-2 minutes, if necessary. Serve with the skin facing upwards and a citrus wedge.

browned fish

serves 1

vegetable oil
1 salmon fillet, preferably
  from the middle,
  weighing about 125g
salt and freshly ground
  black pepper
lemon or lime wedges,
  to serve

Lightly brush or wipe a flat, non-stick dish with vegetable oil and put in the salmon flesh-side up. Brush very lightly with vegetable oil if you wish (salmon is an oily fish) and season with salt and freshly ground black pepper. Cook at 250°C/260°C at the top of the oven for 7–8 minutes, until the surface is well browned and nicely crisp. Test for doneness by inserting a small knife and separating the flakes. Continue cooking for another 1–2 minutes, if necessary. Serve with the flesh facing upwards and a wedge of citrus fruit.

Hearty, rustic and quite complex in flavour, this stew is quick to cook and very easy to prepare. What I like best about it is the browning flavours you can taste in the vegetables, which would be hard to get from any other cooking method. Use whatever large white fish is available.

fish stew with potatoes and fennel

serves 4

1 large potato, cut into
   2.5cm chunks
1 tablespoon vegetable oil
salt and freshly ground
   black pepper
1 large onion, cut into
   2.5cm chunks
2 fennel bulbs, cut into
   generous 1cm slices
   (save the fronds for
   garnish if they are nice
   and fresh)
2 plump garlic cloves,
   thinly sliced
1 x 400g tin chopped
   tomatoes
1 bay leaf
1 large piece each of
   lemon and orange peel
pinch each of fennel
   seeds, dried thyme and
   dried tarragon
large pinch of saffron
75ml dry white wine
600g boneless round fish
   (e.g. hake, cod, pollack
   or whiting), cut into
   large chunks

Toss the potato and oil very thoroughly in an ovenproof casserole about 12.5cm deep and 25cm in diameter. Season well with salt and lots of freshly ground black pepper. Cook at 200°C at the top of the oven, stirring a few times, until the potatoes have taken on a good colour, about 10 minutes. Add the onion, fennel and garlic. Toss them well and cook for another 5 minutes or so with a couple of good stirs; the aim is to colour the vegetables lightly.

Now add the tomatoes, bay leaf, lemon and orange zest, fennel seeds, dried herbs, saffron and wine. Stir very well and continue cooking, stirring a few times, until the potatoes are just cooked, about 10 minutes. Don't worry if the tomatoes get darkened; this is a good thing. But if the liquid is cooking down too much, add a little wine or water.

Now remove the dish from the oven and add the fish, stirring it in gently so as not to break up the flesh. Cook until the fish is just done, stirring a few times, about 5–10 minutes. Top with the fennel fronds, if using, and serve with a green salad or some plainly steamed or roasted vegetables.

The size of the halogen oven means that you're limited in the size of fish you can cook whole. But you can overcome some of the limitation by adapting a technique used by Chinese cooks when steaming. Instead of laying the fish out flat, curl it in the baking dish.

whole baked fish

serves 4

1 large trout, medium-sized sea bass or very small salmon, weighing about 1kg
vegetable oil
3 spring onions, finely chopped
2 thick slices ginger, peeled and finely chopped
2 plump garlic cloves, finely chopped
2 tablespoons soy sauce
2 teaspoons sesame oil
small handful of fresh coriander, chopped

Rub the fish all over with vegetable oil and stuff the spring onions, ginger and garlic into the cavity. Curl the fish to fit inside a heavy baking dish, with the opening of the cavity facing down. Cook at 200°C in the middle of the oven for about 25 minutes, until just done. In the meantime, whisk the soy sauce and sesame oil together. Serve a little of the stuffing with each portion and sprinkle each piece with the soy sauce and sesame oil mixture, plus a little chopped coriander. Steamed rice completes the picture.

This recipe, a variant of the one above, makes a fantastic dinner that is ready in barely ten minutes, including preparation time. Use small whiting, trout, hake, mackerel – any round fish of the right size.

fish dinner for two

serves 2

2 whole fish, weighing about 250g apiece
1 small onion, sliced
8–12 cherry tomatoes
2 lemon quarters
salt and freshly ground black pepper
1 tablespoon extra virgin olive oil
6–8 sprigs of parsley, finely chopped

Curl the fish around the perimeter of a heavy, flat-bottomed dish at least 26cm in diameter, or just lay them flat in the dish. Put the onion slices, tomatoes and lemon quarters in the centre. Season with salt and freshly ground black pepper, then sprinkle the oil over the fish and vegetables. Cook at 200°C at the middle of the oven for 7–10 minutes, until the fish is just cooked. Serve out between you, garnish with parsley and squeeze the juice from the hot lemon quarters over your food before digging in.

poultry

Poultry is one of the halogen oven's favourite food groups. This is great news for people who enjoy really good chicken, because they will love what it does in the halogen oven. Pieces of fairly uniform thickness perform brilliantly, cooking evenly in sometimes astonishingly short times. You can go from cold and raw to cooked and crisp in as little as ten minutes, and adding an extra ten to those timings will give you most of the dishes in this chapter. Other poultry – especially quail and duck – are also prime candidates. And the dishes are by no means all simple grills: chicken pie is perfect under halogen and roast chicken was never quicker. As always with chicken, it is important to cook it thoroughly.

A straightforward preparation with knock-out results. You can of course add whatever spices, herbs and seasonings you like with a roast chicken.

roast chicken and some vegetables

serves 4

1 plump garlic clove, peeled
top-notch chicken, weighing about 1.5kg
salt and freshly ground black pepper
vegetable oil
4–5 celery stalks, cut into pieces about 7.5cm long
4–5 carrots, halved or quartered lengthwise and cut into pieces about 7.5cm long

Stick the garlic in the cavity of the chicken and season the cavity however you want to. Put it, breast down, on whichever roasting rack will raise it to mid-level in the oven, and rub all over with vegetable oil. Set aside. Scatter the vegetables in the bottom of the oven and toss them with a little vegetable oil. Put the prepared chicken into the oven, making sure all feet of the rack are placed securely on the base. The chicken should be no closer to the element than 10cm or so; use the extender ring if you need to.

Cook the chicken at 200°C, occasionally basting the breast with pan juices (use a bulb baster), until it's well browned on top, about 30 minutes. Turn it, using wooden spoons so as not to break the skin. Continue cooking until the skin is crisp and the chicken is just done, about another 30 minutes or so.

Remove the chicken and leave it to rest for at least 15 minutes. In the meantime, remove the extender ring and continue cooking the vegetables at 250°C/260°C so they soften and take on a nicely browned colour.

This recipe yields a main course as well as a side dish because the celery provides enough vegetable matter for a meal. Serve with rice or potatoes to complete the picture.

tarragon chicken with celery and mushrooms

serves 4

few sprigs of fresh
   tarragon or ½ teaspoon
   dried tarragon
2 tablespoons dry white
   wine
1 plump garlic clove,
   finely chopped
6–8 celery stalks, thinly
   sliced on the bias
salt and freshly ground
   black pepper
4 chicken pieces, leg or
   breast
1 tablespoon vegetable oil
75ml chicken stock
100g small button
   mushrooms, whole

Put the tarragon, wine, garlic and celery in a deep dish, season with salt and freshly ground black pepper, and toss well. Put in the chicken pieces (breasts with flesh sides facing up), and brush them with the oil. Set the dish on a rack in the middle of the oven and cook at 250°C/260°C for 10–15 minutes, or until the chicken is lightly browned. Turn the chicken and continue cooking until the skin is crisp and the flesh, just done, about 10 minutes or so more.

Remove the chicken to a serving dish and leave it to rest for a few minutes. In the meantime, add the stock and mushrooms to the deep dish and cook at 250°C/260°C until the liquid is bubbling and the mushrooms are cooked al dente. Spoon the sauce and vegetables over the chicken pieces to serve.

This dish is ready to eat in the time it takes to cook the rice that serves its divinely ordained partner.

chicken in soy sauce

serves 2–3

2 large chicken legs or breasts, cut into 5cm chunks, preferably through the bone (your butcher can do this for you if you don't have a cleaver)
freshly ground black pepper
2 tablespoons soy sauce
1 tablespoon vegetable oil

2 plump garlic cloves, finely chopped
2 thick slices of fresh ginger, peeled and finely chopped
large pinch of Chinese five-spice powder (optional)
1 teaspoon sesame oil
2 spring onions, coarsely chopped

Place the chicken chunks in a large, flat dish and grind on plenty of black pepper. Toss thoroughly with all remaining ingredients except the sesame oil and spring onions. Leave to marinate for a couple of hours, or overnight if possible.

Place in the oven near the top and cook at 200°C for 15–20 minutes, turning once.

Drizzle over the sesame oil, sprinkle with the chopped spring onions and serve with rice.

Instead of using the spices, you can substitute your favourite curry powder. Marinating the chicken overnight, or all day, works wonders.

chicken in spicy yogurt

serves 2

2 boneless chicken breasts or 4 thighs, skin removed
125ml Bio or Greek-style yogurt
1 tablespoon vegetable oil
pinch each of ground cumin, ground coriander, mild chilli powder, salt, freshly ground black pepper and turmeric
coriander leaves, to garnish

Cut deep slashes into the chicken at roughly 2.5cm intervals. Whisk the yogurt, oil and spices together thoroughly, then rub the mixture all over the chicken. Make sure you get the marinade down deep into each incision for maximum flavour penetration. Cover and refrigerate for at least 30 minutes but preferably overnight or all day. If marinating for a longer period, try to turn the chicken pieces and spoon over any marinade that has fallen off.

Place the pieces on a flat dish and cook at 200°C at the top of the oven for about 10 minutes (thighs) or 15 minutes (if the breasts are very thick). Turn once during cooking. You can put a little water in the dish if the yogurt mixture seems to be burning. Serve with basmati rice or pitta bread (see page 118).

This is an all-in-one meal for two, needing only some boiled potatoes or rice, which can be cooked in the time it takes to finish the chicken. The crunch and browning flavours are the best bits of this dish.

chicken and fennel

serves 2

3 small or 2 larger fennel
   bulbs, untrimmed
1 small onion, thinly
   sliced
3 tablespoons dry white
   wine
1 tablespoon vegetable oil
salt and freshly ground
   pepper
2 chicken legs (jointed
   into drumstick and
   thigh) or breasts
small handful of dill, to
   garnish (optional)

Trim the fennel, setting aside the frilly fronds as a garnish and chopping them finely. (If the fronds are not fresh and green and of good quality, you may want to use dill as a garnish instead.) Slice the bulbs crosswise into thin pieces.

Toss the fennel, onion, wine and oil in a large, flat dish with 2 tablespoons of water and season with salt and freshly ground black pepper. Cook at 200°C at the middle of the oven for 5 minutes or so, just until the fennel is starting to look a little bit cooked. Toss it once or twice during cooking.

Now put the chicken on top of the fennel (thighs with the flesh side facing up). Cook for 10 minutes or so, until it's well browned. Turn and cook until the skin is well browned and crisp, and the flesh is just cooked (another 10 minutes for legs, perhaps a bit longer for very thick breasts). The fennel slices that haven't been covered by chicken will be browned and slightly blackened in places.

Serve the chicken with the fennel on the side and some potatoes or rice as a starchy accompaniment. The fennel fronds or dill should be scattered freely on top just before serving.

Boning a chicken is hard, but boning chicken thighs is easy. If you disagree, be nice to your butcher and he or she will do it for you. The stuffing can be any tasty combination you like; I have given three ideas at the end of the recipe. In all cases, the dish will benefit from being stuffed in advance and left for a while. (Think of it as marinating from the inside.) This is easy enough for a midweek supper but impressive enough for a dinner party.

stuffed chicken thighs

serves 4

8 smallish chicken thighs, boned
salt and freshly ground black pepper
stuffing of your choice (see below)
45ml dry white wine
vegetable oil

Lay the thighs, flesh side facing up, on a chopping board or another flat, clean surface. Season with salt and freshly ground black pepper, then divide the stuffing between the thighs, laying it in the indentation where the bone used to be. Roll each thigh up tightly and place, seam-side down, in a large, flat-bottomed dish. (This recipe may be prepared in advance up to this point and refrigerated, covered.)

Pour the wine in the dish, brush the skin all over with vegetable oil and cook at 200°C at the top of the oven until the chicken's just done and the skin is nicely brown, about 15 minutes. Serve with rice or mashed potatoes.

Stuffing options
• Large handful of coriander, finely chopped; 2–3 spring onions, finely chopped; 2–3 slices of ginger, peeled and finely chopped
• Small onion, finely chopped; 1 red chilli, finely chopped; large pinch of dried oregano; few drops of dry white wine and red wine vinegar
• Large handful of parsley, finely chopped; few shreds of lemon zest, finely chopped; 1 small garlic clove, finely chopped; pinch of dried thyme

To release more of the lemongrass flavour, bruise it with the flat side of the blade of a heavy knife or a cleaver. Longer marinating, up to eight hours, lifts this dish to another level.

chicken wings with red curry paste

serves 3–4

450g chicken wings (tips cut off and saved for stock), and jointed
2 tablespoons Thai red curry paste
1 tablespoon vegetable oil
1 plump garlic clove, crushed or finely chopped
1 shallot or ½ small onion, finely chopped
1 lemongrass stalk, bruised and cut in 5cm lengths
coriander leaves, to garnish
lemon or lime wedges, to serve

Mix all ingredients except the coriander leaves and citrus wedges in a bowl. The easiest way to do this is using your hands, which will need a vigorous scrub afterwards. If the wings need more oil – you can tell by whether they are easily tossed in the marinade – add up to another tablespoon. Cover and refrigerate for at least an hour, but 8 or more would be better.

Put the wings in a flat dish that will hold them in a single layer. Cook at 250°C/260°C in the middle of the oven, turning once or twice. They should need 10–15 minutes to reach moderate colour and full juiciness, but another 5 minutes will get more colour and more crunch into the skin. If you cook them at grilling level, the skin will become even more delectably crisp, but the cooking will be a couple of minutes shorter. Garnish with coriander leaves and serve with wedges of lime or lemon.

variation

My brother, Henry, does something similar using liberal coatings of a favoured spice mixture – 'jerk or curry or anything, and some coarse salt'. Refrigerate for an hour, then cook at 200°C at the middle of the oven for 20 minutes. Then turn the chicken and cook for another 5 minutes. He also says, 'As a variation, you can baste them after 15 with a barbecue sauce, tamarind chutney or anything else like that, then give them 5 more on each side. This is a good way to dole out a lot of party food in a hurry.' The chicken wings are just as good at room temperature as they are straight-from-the-oven hot.

This makes a great midweek supper for two. Serve the burgers on a roll or on their own, with a yogurt sauce, such as raita, to cool the burn from the chilli. The courgettes moisten the burgers, so take care when turning them. This recipe can be made for up to four by doubling the quantities and moving the burgers around during cooking. You could also make these burgers using minced turkey.

spicy chicken and courgette burger

serves 2–3

250g minced chicken, preferably from the thigh

1 smallish courgette, weighing about 75g, coarsely grated

1 small red chilli, deseeded if you wish, and finely chopped

1–2 slices of fresh ginger, peeled and finely chopped

1 plump garlic clove, finely chopped

salt and freshly ground black pepper

plain flour

vegetable oil

Mix the chicken and courgette with the rest of the ingredients except the flour and oil, and season with salt and freshly ground black pepper. Form the mixture into 2 balls and roll them in the flour. Then flatten them into patties about 2.5cm thick. Lightly, but not completely, coat the bottom of a thin metal dish with a little vegetable oil. Put the patties into the dish and place it in grilling position in the oven. Cook at 250°C/260°C until the patties are well browned on top, about 10 minutes.

Lift out the burgers with a spatula and turn them over. Continue cooking about 5–10 minutes more, until the second side is well browned and the meat is cooked right through. Serve immediately on a roll of your choice, with some salad leaves and onion slices, if you wish.

This simple dish, which can be made with either legs or breasts, illustrates perfectly the half-roasting, half-grilling capability of the halogen oven. These measurements are per person, as the dish takes no more time to cook for four than for one.

herb and pepper duck

serves 1

1 duck quarter, leg or
   breast
pinch of dried mixed
   herbs, such as herbes
   de Provence
large pinch of coarsely
   ground black pepper
salt, coarse or fine

Put the duck in a flat metal cooking dish, skin side facing down. Mix the herbs and ground pepper together and spread them as evenly as possible on the flesh side of the duck piece. Leave for at least an hour, but preferably for 4 hours or more, covered, in the fridge.

When you're ready to cook, sprinkle the duck lightly with coarse or fine salt. Press the salt into the flesh, then turn the pieces over so the skin side is facing up. Set the dish at the middle of the oven and cook at 200°C for 15 minutes. Then turn the temperature up to 250°C/260°C.Cook for another 3–5 minutes, until the skin is crisp and the flesh firm to the touch and lightly browned. If you're cooking more than 2 pieces of duck, move them around halfway through cooking so they all get a spell sitting right under the element. Leave the duck to rest for a few minutes before serving.

The compact and even shape of a duck breast means it benefits from a blast of fierce grilling heat. These timings are for medium-rare duck – cooked all the way through but with a hint of pink at the centre.

speedy duck breast

serves 1

1 duck breast
pinch of dried mixed
 herbs, such as herbes
 de Provence
large pinch of coarsely
 ground black pepper
coarse or fine salt

Put the duck in a flat metal cooking dish, skin side facing down. Mix the herbs and ground pepper together and spread them as evenly as possible on the flesh side of the duck breast. Leave for at least an hour, but preferably for 4 hours or more, covered, in the fridge.

When you're ready to cook, sprinkle the duck lightly with salt, coarse or fine. Press the salt into the flesh, then cook with the flesh side facing up at 250°C/260°C at the top of the oven. Cook until the flesh is nicely browned, (about 5–7 minutes), then turn and keep cooking for another 4–5 minutes, until the skin is well browned and deeply crisp. If you're cooking more than 2 duck breasts, move them around halfway during cooking so that all of them get a spell sitting right under the element. Leave the duck to rest for a few minutes before serving.

Quail, those expensive but tasty little birds, are
perfect candidates for cooking in the halogen oven.

quail with onions, olives and cherry tomatoes

serves 2 as a main
course, 4 as a starter

1 medium onion, cut into
   thick slices
good knob of butter
50ml dry white wine
½ teaspoon dried
   rosemary
salt and freshly ground
   black pepper
4 oven-ready quail
8 big fat green olives,
   pitted
8 cherry tomatoes
2 teaspoons concentrated
   chicken stock or wine
   (optional)

Put the onions, butter and wine in a large, flat-bottomed dish. Place at the top of the oven and cook at 250°C/260°C until the butter melts. Toss well and continue cooking just until the onions take on a bit of colour, about 5 minutes. Sprinkle on the dried rosemary and season with a little salt and plenty of freshly ground black pepper. Place the quail on top, on their sides, doing your best to cover the onions completely. Cook at 200°C for 5 minutes. Then turn them over and cook on the other side for another 5 minutes.

Turn the quail so the breasts face up. Cook until the breast is lightly browned and the birds are fully cooked, about 10 minutes.

Remove the quail from the cooking dish to a heated plate or platter. Put the olives and tomatoes in the dish and cook for 1–2 minutes, just to heat them through.

The liquid from the tomatoes, onions and wine will produce a few spoonfuls of juice to moisten the quail. If you require more, a spoonful or two of concentrated chicken stock or a little extra wine will do the trick. Mashed potatoes are the ideal accompaniment here.

a cure for skinny legs

Some birds, notably guinea fowl, wood pigeon and pheasant, have very skinny, flat legs that cook in next to no time. If you have the birds jointed for serving the breasts only, the legs can be put to excellent use in very fast-cooking meals. Put them in a flat-bottomed metal dish with a little vegetable oil, season, then cook for 8–10 minutes (guinea fowl and pheasant) or 5–6 minutes (wood pigeon) in grilling position at 250°C/260°C.

Don't be put off by the number of ingredients or the length of this recipe. This rich dish is dead easy and well worth making for a family supper. Here's a hint: the stock must be hot when it goes in to prevent clumping of the flour.

chicken and mushroom pie with a cobbler crust

serves 4–6

2–3 celery stalks, sliced
1 small onion, finely chopped
1 tablespoon vegetable oil
salt and freshly ground
   black pepper
1 tablespoon plain flour
250ml hot chicken stock
½ teaspoon dried herbs
   (tarragon, oregano
   or herbes de Provence)
4 large or 8 small chicken
   thighs, skinned, boned
   and quartered
300g button mushrooms,
   cleaned and halved (if
   necessary)
100ml double cream or
   crème fraîche

For the cobbler topping
150g self-raising flour
75g butter, cut into
   small pieces
½ teaspoon dried herbs
   (tarragon, oregano or
   herbes de Provence), or
   a very small handful of
   fresh (tarragon or thyme
   are top choices)
salt and freshly ground
   black pepper
60ml semi skimmed or
   whole milk
1 tablespoon single cream
   (optional)

Put the celery and onion in a round or square ovenproof dish at least 7.5cm deep. (The dish should fit in the oven with at least 2.5cm between it and the oven wall, so the hot air can circulate.) Toss with about 1 tablespoon of oil, just enough to coat them lightly. Season and cook at 250°C/260°C at the top of the oven until slightly softened and coloured, about 10 minutes. Once they're softened, stir in the flour and continue cooking for a minute more, then pour in the hot stock and the herbs. Continue cooking at a low heat, just to keep the mixture hot until the cobbler mixture is ready.

In the meantime, make the cobbler topping. Put the flour and butter in a mixing bowl and work the butter in as quickly as possible until the mixture resembles coarse breadcrumbs; you can do this with two knives or your fingertips. Add the herbs and season with salt and plenty of freshly ground black pepper. Pour in the milk and cream (if using) and blend thoroughly but quickly. It's important not to overwork the mixture or the topping won't rise as well as it should. The aim is to have a firm but fairly sticky dough, so if you're not using the cream, you may want to add more milk.

Set the chicken pieces on top of the vegetables and cook at 250°C/260°C to brown lightly, about 5 minutes. Add the mushrooms and cream or crème fraîche, stir quickly and continue cooking for 5 minutes more. Top the chicken mixture evenly with blobs of cobbler dough by using a pair of spoons or just scraping it off a spoon with your fingers or a knife, about 1 tablespoonful at a time, leaving spaces between the blobs.

Cook at 200°C until the topping is well browned and cooked through, about 15–20 minutes. The liquid should be bubbling merrily. Leave to rest for a couple of minutes before serving with plain green vegetables. The pie is quite rich so nothing oily or buttery is needed.

meat

I've concentrated on relatively simple dishes here – some roasted, some grilled and some cooked with that combination of roasting and grilling that is the hallmark of the halogen oven. The speed in some of these dishes is mind-blowing – look particularly at the roast beef if you need proof. I've also tried braising meat in the halogen oven. The results, though passable, were not good enough to sway me from a conviction that the oven's at its best with dry heat on simple cuts with a fairly flat, uniform surface. There are exceptions here, however. For example, there's a recipe for something akin to a stir-fry, as well as steak wrapped around a savoury stuffing, which works beautifully.

roast pork in two sizes

Cooking a very small joint of anything in the conventional oven is difficult: the short cooking time needed may not be sufficient to brown the skin and transform the skin into crackling. However, the halogen oven comes to the rescue with both these problems through its combination of roasting and grilling. The ideal cut here is a piece of rolled shoulder from the thin end of the shoulder, or boneless loin.

small size

serves 2–3

small pork joint, about
  7.5cm thick (300–450g)
vegetable oil
salt and freshly ground
  black pepper

Put the joint on a roasting rack over an ovenproof plate. Rub the pork all over with vegetable oil, salt and pepper.

Set the dish in the oven so the meat is about 10cm from the heating element and cook at 250°C/260°C for 5 minutes. Turn the heat down to 200°C and cook for another 10 minutes. Turn the meat over and repeat those timings. Then turn the roast so the skin side is facing the element. If you need to, you can prop it up between 2 ovenproof ramekins or something similar. Cook it for a few minutes more to crisp up the skin. Leave it to rest (10 minutes should do it) before slicing.

a note on roasts

For all the roasts found on the next few pages, dried herbs, especially oregano, sage or rosemary, will make a good addition to the salt, pepper and vegetable oil rub. You can reduce cooking times by 10 per cent or more if the meat is at room temperature when it goes into the oven. This means taking it out of the fridge at least two hours before you roast it.

For a larger joint, a thick piece of belly is perfect, as is a boned and rolled loin from the thin end of the loin.

medium size

serves 3–4

medium-sized pork joint, about 10cm thick (600–750g)
vegetable oil
salt and freshly ground black pepper

Put the joint on a roasting rack over an ovenproof plate and rub all over with vegetable oil, salt and freshly ground black pepper. Cook at 250°C/250°C at the bottom of the oven until it is done medium rare (or well done, if you must). The time needed should be no more than 35 minutes and maybe as little as 25.

The only trick here is that with certain joints, such as boned and rolled loin, you need to turn the pork as it's cooking so all the skin gets crackled and no one surface gets blackened by the halogen element. Just keep an eye on the joint and turn regularly – 4 or 5 times during cooking should do the trick. As always with roast meat, leave it to rest (10 minutes should be fine) before slicing.

Cooking a thick and irregular chunk of meat in the halogen oven is always trickier than cooking something that's thin and/or of uniform thickness. But it can be done, and this leg of lamb proves it. The shank end of the leg must be cut off to around midway up its length, so the joint will fit in the oven. Needless to say, you should freeze the shank for another day – it will feed two people easily. The leg itself will feed four or six happy diners.

Please note: joints like this vary greatly in size and thickness, and the variables here are formidable. Use my timings as a guideline only. And if you have another way of seasoning lamb that you prefer to mine, use yours. Note finally: you will have to get your butcher's cooperation in cutting up the leg, unless you happen to own a butcher's saw.

leg of lamb with mustard, anchovies and garlic

serves 4

1 leg of lamb, about
    3kg in weight, shank
    trimmed
1 tablespoon plain flour
2 tablespoons French
    mustard
1 tablespoon anchovy
    paste or finely chopped
    anchovies in oil
1 tablespoon extra virgin
    olive oil
2 garlic cloves, finely
    chopped
freshly ground black
    pepper

Trim the lamb of excess fat if necessary, and set aside. Mix all the other ingredients together and rub them over the joint. Refrigerate for at least 6 hours and preferably overnight. Bring to room temperature before cooking by leaving out of the fridge for at least 2 hours.

Position the lamb in the oven so it is at least 12.5cm away from the element; this will almost certainly require use of the extender ring. Cook for 15 minutes at 250°C/260°C, then for 30 minutes at 200°C. Turn and give it 15 minutes at 250°C/260°C, then 25–30 minutes at 200°C. Leave to rest for at least 15 minutes and a maximum of 30. The outer regions will be well done but not dried out; the zone underneath that will be medium; and the innermost portions will range from pink-rare to medium-rare.

The cut to use here is a piece of shoulder, boned and left unrolled. You will be amazed at how fast it cooks, especially if you leave it to come to room temperature before cooking.

lightning-quick lamb joint

serves 4–6

boned shoulder of lamb (about 1.75kg on the bone), no more than 5cm thick at its thickest point
1–2 plump garlic cloves, thinly sliced
2 teaspoons dried rosemary, crumbled
1 tablespoon vegetable oil
salt and freshly ground black pepper

Trim excess fat from the meat. Put the garlic slices in a flat metal dish and lay the lamb on top. Mix the rosemary and oil with a good dose of salt and freshly ground black pepper and rub thoroughly all over the joint. This dish may be prepared in advance up to this point and refrigerated, covered, to allow the herbs to act as a dry marinade. Leaving it overnight would be ideal.

Cook at 250°C/260°C at the top of the oven until the uppermost surface of the meat is well browned and it is cooked to medium-rare (a modest hint of pink) in its thickest area. This will take 10–15 minutes if the lamb is thin (up to 3.5cm) and 15–20 minutes if it is thicker. As always, leave to rest for about 10 minutes before slicing.

Note: you can make the dry rub more interesting using ground spices mixed with garlic, for example, but it's best to sprinkle this on towards the end of cooking. This is because the high heat can burn the spices and make them taste bitter.

I tried this wonderful cut several times in the halogen oven before spotting the best way forward. If you use a whole rack (seven to eight cutlets), the cooking is uneven because the end cutlets get less heat than those in the middle. The solution: cut the rack into portions of two to four cutlets each (depending on the size of the racks). Then you can switch the mini-racks so those under the element move to the outside and vice versa. It takes a bit of watching and fiddling, but the lamb cooks so quickly, with such succulent results, you won't mind. Note: placing a few garlic cloves around the lamb will give you a pungent morsel to serve on the side.

rack of lamb

for two-cutlet racks

serves 2–4

vegetable oil
4 mini-racks of lamb,
   with 2 cutlets in a
   single rack
salt and freshly ground
   black pepper

Lightly oil a flat, non-stick cooking dish. Put the lamb racks in with the fat side facing up and season with salt and freshly ground black pepper. Cook at 250°C/260°C near the top of the oven, switching the pieces around so those under the element move to the outside, and vice versa, until they're lightly browned, about 3 minutes. Turn them on one side, season lightly, and cook until the meat is well browned, about 3 minutes. Turn onto the other side, season lightly, and cook again until well browned, about another 3 minutes. Finally, turn them so the underside is facing up and cook until well browned, about another 3 minutes. Turn so the fat side is facing up and cook just for another minute or so, to crisp up fully. Leave to rest for 5 minutes before serving.

for three- or four-cutlet racks

serves 4

vegetable oil
4 mini-racks of lamb,
   with 3–4 cutlets in a
   single rack
salt and freshly ground
   black pepper

Lightly oil a flat, non-stick cooking dish. Put the lamb racks in with the fat side facing up and season with salt and freshly ground black pepper. Cook at 250°C/260°C near the top of the oven, switching the pieces around so those under the element move to the outside, and vice versa, until they're well browned, about 5–6 minutes. Turn them over and cook until well browned, about another 5–6 minutes. Finally, turn them so the fat side is facing up and cook just for another minute or so, to crisp up fully. Leave to rest for 5 minutes before serving.

Note: to do individual lamb cutlets, cook at 250°C/260°C in grilling position, switching the pieces around so those under the element move to the outside, and vice versa, for 3–4 minutes on the first side (until well browned) and about 2 minutes on the second side.

The halogen oven cooks a good rib of beef so fast and so well you'll never want to use the conventional oven again. That is, as long as you're not cooking more than two ribs, because the oven simply can't accommodate more than two at a time. But that shouldn't be too much of a drawback, because the larger-sized roast described here can still serve up to eight.

rib of beef in two sizes

small size

serves 3–4

1 teaspoon herbes de Provence
1 teaspoon freshly coarsely ground black pepper
single rib of well-hung beef, about 5cm thick, weighing about 1–1.3kg
1 teaspoon coarse salt

Mix the herbs and pepper together and rub into both sides of the beef. Leave to sit, unrefrigerated, for at least 2 hours so the flavour of the seasonings can penetrate the flesh a little and the beef itself come to room temperature. When you're ready to cook, rub the salt in and place the beef on a wire rack. Cook at the middle of the oven at 200°C, turning once, until it's done the way you like it: 20 minutes for rare; 25 for medium-rare. Anything more than medium-rare and you're ruining the meat.

larger size

serves 6–8

1 teaspoon herbes de Provence
1 teaspoon coarsely freshly ground black pepper
double rib of well-hung beef, about 10cm thick, weighing about 2–2.6kg
1 teaspoon coarse salt

Mix the herbs and pepper together and rub into both sides of the beef. Leave to sit, unrefrigerated, for at least 2 hours so the flavour of the seasonings can penetrate the flesh a little and the beef itself come to room temperature. When you're ready to cook, rub the salt in and place the beef on a wire rack. Place the rack so it is at the bottom of the oven, about 12.5cm from the heating element. Cook at 200°C for 40 minutes, then turn it over using a pair of carving forks or metal serving spoons. Cook for another 20 minutes for rare, 25 for medium-rare. Anything more than medium-rare and you're ruining the meat.

Note: when the oven has been on for an hour, even the plastic can get hot. Be careful.

The watercress is merely wilted in the heat of the cooked dish, preserving nearly all of its crunch.

oriental beef and vegetables

serves 2–3

250g lean steak, cut into thick strips
1 plump garlic clove, finely chopped
1 fresh chilli, finely chopped
1 spring onion, finely chopped
1 tablespoon soy sauce
2 teaspoons oyster sauce
2 teaspoons red wine vinegar

4 celery stalks, trimmed and thinly sliced
1 large red or yellow pepper, deseeded and thinly sliced
1 tablespoon vegetable oil
freshly ground black pepper
2 teaspoons sesame oil
1 bunch watercress, thick stems removed

Marinate the steak in the garlic, chilli, spring onions, sauces and vinegar for 1–4 hours.

Toss the celery and pepper with the oil and lots of black pepper in a flat metal dish. Cook in grilling position at 250°C/260°C, stirring once or twice, until lightly coloured in places and slightly softened, about 7–8 minutes. Scatter the beef on top and continue cooking until the beef is just done, about 3 minutes. Remove to a serving bowl, stir in the sesame oil and watercress, and toss well. Serve with boiled rice.

This can be beef, pork or lamb. With pork mince, ensure it is cooked medium at the very least. If you are using lamb, medium-rare is ideal. But if it is beef you are using, follow your own path.

the essential burger

serves 1

100–150g minced meat
salt and freshly ground black pepper

Form the meat into a patty 2.5cm thick. Season with salt and pepper. Cook in grilling position at 250°C/260°C on a rack or in a flat-bottomed dish until well browned on top (5–6 minutes). Then turn and cook for another 2 minutes for rare, 3–4 minutes for medium-rare, 4–5 minutes for medium or 6 minutes for well done.

Embellishing the essential burger
Try adding any of the following to the mince mix before grilling:
• a few sprigs of parsley or coriander, finely chopped
• a slice of onion, finely chopped
• a little chilli, finely chopped
• a little garlic, finely chopped
• a few drops of Worcestershire or soy sauce

Rolling slices of meat around a stuffing is a well-loved procedure in both French and Italian cooking. It may sound tricky, but it's actually very simple as long as you have a thin enough piece of meat. The best way to get it is by buying a steak about 1cm thick and pounding it thin with a meat mallet (or an empty wine bottle, if you don't have a mallet). This recipe uses duxelles (see page 33), one of the home cook's greatest allies, as the stuffing.

rolled steak with duxelles

serves 4

4 thin steaks, either
   rump, sirloin or feather
120g duxelles
   (see page 33)
vegetable oil

Pound the steaks to about 6mm thick and 10 x 20cm in size, then set aside. Lightly oil a flat, non-stick cooking dish. Spread one-quarter of the duxelles over each steak, leaving a gap of about 1cm between the duxelles and the edge of the steak. Neatly roll up the steak, starting at the edge with the duxelles. Place the roll in the dish, seam-side down. Repeat with the remaining 3 steaks. Don't crowd the steak rolls together on the dish, and aim to have two rolls right at the centre, so they'll be directly under the element in the oven.

Brush the tops of the rolls lightly with vegetable oil. Cook at 250°C/260°C at grilling level for 3 minutes, then switch the rolls so those under the element move to the outside, and vice versa. Cook until the stuffing is hot and the beef is cooked to medium-rare. This will take another 3–4 minutes if the rolls are on the thin side, but could take as much as 5–7 minutes if they're thick. You might find that the top is cooked more than the bottom, but no one will mind.

The rolls can be served with new potatoes and salad or set right onto a bed of rice or mashed potatoes.

Mmmm, meatloaf. The best variety to cook under halogen is a free-form loaf, rather than the classic cooked in a loaf tin. In this recipe, the meat is formed into a mound around 5cm deep. Done that way, the quantities can be doubled if you're feeding a larger crowd.

free-form meatloaf

serves 2 with some
left over, 3 easily,
and 4 or 5 at a pinch

2 celery stalks, trimmed and coarsely chopped
1 medium onion, coarsely chopped
2 teaspoons vegetable oil (optional)
450g beef, not too lean (about 20 per cent fat would be good)
large handful of fresh breadcrumbs or cooked white rice
1 free-range egg, beaten
3 strips of streaky bacon, rinds removed and cut into 1cm lardons
½ teaspoon dried oregano
salt and freshly ground black pepper

If you want to make sure the celery and onions are really soft (some people prefer them that way in meatloaf), mix them on a flat metal dish with the vegetable oil and cook them at 200°C in the middle of the oven for 4–5 minutes. Leave to cool before mixing with all the other ingredients.

If you're not pre-cooking the vegetables, simply mix all the ingredients (minus the vegetable oil) either in a mixing bowl or on a flat metal dish you can then use for cooking the meatloaf (saves on washing up). Season well with salt and freshly ground black pepper. Form into a mound about 5cm high at its highest point. You can try to square up the sides for a neater appearance, but the mound gives a meatloaf that's more well done at the periphery, and some people like meatloaf to be well done while others like it more medium-rare.

Bake at 250°C/260°C in the middle of the oven for 10 minutes. Turn down the heat to 200°C and bake for 10 minutes more. Leave to rest for a couple of minutes before slicing if serving hot, or leave to cool completely if slicing for sandwiches.

This is perfect for a midweek supper or an informal dinner party dish.

spicy stuffed peppers

serves 4

400–500g minced pork, lamb, beef or chicken (dark meat only)
200g cooked rice or fresh breadcrumbs
1 celery stalk, trimmed and coarsely chopped
1 free-range egg, beaten
1 medium onion, coarsely chopped
1 tablespoon tomato ketchup or tomato sauce
1 teaspoon chilli sauce

large pinch of dried herbs, such as thyme or oregano, or use herbes de Provence
2 tablespoons extra virgin olive oil
small handful of parsley, finely chopped
salt and freshly ground black pepper
2 large or 4 small red peppers, halved and deseeded
large knob of butter

Put the meat in a mixing bowl and add all remaining ingredients except the peppers and butter. If the meat is very lean, you can add a little more oil. Season with salt and lots of pepper, and blend well.

Put the peppers halves in a flat dish and stuff with the mixture; it doesn't matter if it is mounded high. Dot with the butter and put a splash of water in the dish to keep the bottoms from catching. Cook at 200°C at the bottom of the oven until the meat is fully cooked and the top nicely browned, about 20–25 minutes.

The traditional terrine dish is not ideal for the halogen oven because the top can get too brown before the meat has cooked at the bottom. Use a flat metal dish instead – you'll get thinner slices, but no one will complain.

bacon and pork terrine

serves 6–8

2 plump garlic cloves, finely chopped
1 small onion, finely chopped
2 tablespoons dry white wine
1 teaspoon herbes de Provence
750g ground pork or plain sausage meat, not too lean (about 20 per cent fat would be good)
3 strips of streaky bacon, rinds removed and cut into thick lardons
salt and freshly ground black pepper

Soften the garlic and onion by cooking them briefly with the wine and the herbs; this is easiest and quickest in the microwave. Or mix them on a flat metal dish and cook them at 200°C in the middle of the oven for 4–5 minutes. Leave to cool before mixing in all the other ingredients.

Season well with salt and freshly ground black pepper, then form a mound about 5cm high at its highest point. Squaring up the sides for a neater appearance is worth the effort.

Bake at 250°C/260°C in the middle of the oven for 10 minutes. Turn down the heat to 200°C and bake 10–15 minutes more, until a skewer poked into the centre of the terrine comes away hot and dry. Leave to cool completely, then refrigerate until needed (an overnight resting period will mellow the flavour). If there are leftovers, they will cook for 2–3 days in the fridge.

starch

Potatoes and root vegetables, such as parsnips, take to the halogen oven like ducks to water, and the energy and time savings, compared with a full-sized conventional oven, are a massive bonus. You can pre-cook the vegetables in some form (boiling or boiling and mashing), or they can go in raw. Some of the most successful approaches involve cutting whole spuds into pieces, either wedges or cubes. The oven is very good at baking potatoes (see page 103) and it also produces outstanding polenta, macaroni cheese and a simple version of Chinese-style crunchy noodles.

Soft polenta is indescribably boring. But give the stuff a good crust under the halogen oven's ferocious grill and, suddenly, it's irresistible. This recipe makes a large batch so you can keep a slab in the fridge and grill or roast a little bit as needed.

herby polenta chips

serves 4

175g medium polenta (cornmeal)
850ml water
½ teaspoon dried mixed herbs, such as herbes de Provence
salt
60ml extra virgin olive oil, plus extra for brushing

Put the polenta, water and herbs in a large bowl, season with about 1 teaspoon of salt, and cook in the microwave at full power for 2 minutes at a time, stirring after each burst. When it is thick enough not to fall from a spoon without a shake (about 10–12 minutes), stir in the oil. Scrape it into a non-stick metal dish, spreading it out to make it roughly even, and leave to cool.

Once it has cooled, cut 16 fat chips of 7.5cm length from the set polenta. Save the rest of the polenta for another meal – it will keep in tiptop shape for a week or so in the fridge. Lightly oil a non-stick, flat-bottomed metal dish and place the chips on it, evenly spaced apart. Cook at 250°C/260°C in grilling position. Turn at least once, until the chips are crisp, golden and beginning to blacken in places, about 15 minutes. If you wish, you can turn them 4 times so each side gets good and brown.

Next time you fry a duck breast, preserve the fat and use it for roasting parsnips.

crunchy parsnips

serves 3–4

1 large parsnip
1–2 tablespoons duck fat or vegetable oil
salt and freshly ground black pepper
1 thick slice red onion, finely chopped
juice of ¼ lemon

Peel the parsnip if you wish, then halve lengthwise and cut out the woody core. Cut into fairly thick slices, about 1cm. Toss well with the duck fat or oil in a suitable flat-bottomed dish and season with salt and pepper. Cook at 200°C at the top of the oven, with regular stirring and tossing. When they're just soft and blackened in places, toss them with the onion and lemon juice, and serve immediately.

roast new potatoes with rosemary and garlic

serves 4

350g new potatoes, all approximately the same size, halved
1 tablespoon vegetable oil or duck fat
1 teaspoon dried rosemary
1 plump garlic clove, finely chopped
salt and freshly ground black pepper

Toss the potatoes with the vegetable oil or duck fat and the dried rosemary in a flat dish large enough to hold them in a single layer. Cook at 200°C at the middle of the oven, turning a few times. They will take about 15–20 minutes. When the spuds are nearly done, add the garlic, season with salt and freshly ground black pepper and let them finish cooking.

Like all discerning Americans, I rank really good hash browns among the world's great potato dishes. The halogen oven does them well without using too much oil. The only necessity is that you use a dish large enough to hold the potatoes in a fairly thin layer. If you're feeding more than two, multiply the quantities as needed and be prepared for a somewhat longer cooking time.

hash browns

serves 2

1 small potato, weighing about 250g, cut into small dice
1 tablespoon vegetable oil
salt and freshly ground black pepper
1 small onion, weighing about 100g, coarsely chopped
parsley, finely chopped, to garnish (optional)

Put the potato and oil in a thin, non-stick, flat-bottomed dish at least 15cm in diameter. Season with salt and freshly ground black pepper and toss thoroughly. Cook at 250°C/260°C at the top of the oven, stirring at least once, until the potatoes are well browned and nearly cooked, about 8 minutes. Stir in the onion and continue to cook, stirring at least once, until the potatoes are fully cooked and blackened in places. You can add a bit of finely chopped parsley or green pepper halfway through cooking if you want to make yourself feel like there's a green vegetable in there somewhere. Serve immediately.

Making these potato wedges couldn't be simpler. The effect is somewhat similar to that of roast potatoes, but with much less oil involved.

potato wedges

serves 4

2 King Edward or Maris Piper potatoes, weighing about 225g apiece, peeled if you wish (I don't) and quartered lengthwise to make thick wedges
2 tablespoons vegetable oil
salt

Rub or brush the potatoes all over with oil; use more if you need to. Place on a thin, flat-bottomed metal dish, one of the flat sides of each wedge facing downwards. Sprinkle with salt. Cook at 250°C/260°C at the middle of the oven for 20–25 minutes, turning twice so that each surface gets some exposure to the high heat from the element. They're done when well browned all over, with crunchy surfaces and a soft interior.

baked potatoes

You can cook up to 4 baked potatoes in the halogen oven at a time, or 6 if they are small. Prick in a few places with a fork, rub lightly with vegetable oil and cook at 200°C at the bottom of the oven for about 1 hour, turning once. As always with a baked potato, you can reduce the cooking time significantly by starting it off in the microwave. Prick with a fork in several places, then cook at full power until the spud is painfully hot to handle (4–8 minutes depending on size and number). Rub with oil and proceed with halogen baking.

Also known as tattie scones in their native Scotland,
potato scones are ready in minutes using a halogen oven.

potato scones

makes 15–20

450g potatoes, peeled and
  thinly sliced
2 tablespoons plain flour
1 small onion, finely
  chopped
salt and freshly ground
  black pepper
vegetable oil

Cover the potatoes with salted water and bring to the boil. Turn the heat down and simmer gently until they are just cooked. Drain well and mash them, then transfer to a mixing bowl and stir in the flour and onion, plus salt and freshly ground black pepper. Form into patties about 5cm thick, place on a flat, non-stick metal dish and brush the top with oil. Cook at 250°C/260°C at the top of the oven for 12–15 minutes, turning once. After turning, they will need another brushing of oil. Be sure to move the scones around so they all get a spell right under the element. They're done when well browned and sizzling hot.

This is a delicious and very simple dish (pictured right) that
has been loosely adapted from a recipe in Deborah Madison's
The Greens Cookbook, the best vegetarian cookery book ever
written. You can use more chilli if you want to – Madison's recipe
uses tons of them.

variation: patatas gordas

makes 15–20

450g potatoes, peeled
  and thinly sliced
150g plain flour
75g mature Cheddar,
  grated
1 small onion, finely
  chopped
1 small red or green
  chilli, finely chopped
salt and freshly ground
  black pepper
vegetable oil

Cover the potatoes with salted water and bring to the boil. Turn the heat down and simmer gently until the potatoes are just cooked. Drain well and mash them (not too smoothly), then transfer to a mixing bowl and leave to cool. Stir in the flour, cheese, onion and chilli, plus salt and freshly ground black pepper. Form into patties about 2.5cm thick, brush with oil and place them, oiled side facing down, on a flat, non-stick metal dish. Now brush the tops with oil.

Cook at 250°C/260°C at the top of the oven for 10–12 minutes, turning once; after turning, the tops may need another brushing of oil. Be sure to move them around so each one gets a spell right under the element. They're done when well browned and sizzling hot.

I love those fried-noodle dishes with a special crispness – a staple in good Chinese restaurants. Getting that result at home is difficult without using lots of oil, but I've devised a halogenic solution requiring very little. It's very good – and dead easy.

crunchy noodles

serves 3–4 as a
side dish

125g thin wheat noodles
3 tablespoons
    vegetable oil
2 thin slices of fresh
    ginger, finely chopped
1 plump garlic clove,
    finely chopped
1 small chilli, finely
    chopped (optional)

Boil some water in a saucepan and cook the noodles according to the instructions on the packet, but using a slightly shorter cooking time. The idea is to remove them just before they are fully cooked. Drain well, then toss immediately with 2 tablespoons of the oil.

In the meantime, cook the ginger, garlic and chilli very briefly in just enough oil to coat them. I find about 40 seconds in the microwave is ideal for this.

Toss the cooked noodles with the ginger mixture, then use the rest of the oil to coat a flat, non-stick metal dish. Spread out the noodles in an even layer and cook at 250°C/260°C at grilling position until they are crisp and showing signs of blackening in spots, about 5 minutes. They can be served now, but you can also invert the noodles onto a plate, turn back into the cooking dish with the underside uppermost, and cook for another 5 minutes to crisp both sides. Serve immediately.

The halogen oven was surely put on earth just for this dish, especially if you're cooking for only two or three people. To guarantee speedy cooking, it is important that you make sure everything is piping hot when you put it in the oven. I promise you: half an hour from start to finish.

macaroni cheese

serves 2–3

generous knob of butter
1 tablespoon plain flour
salt and freshly ground
    black pepper
1 smallish shallot, finely
    chopped
200ml milk
150g mature Cheddar,
    grated
2 tablespoons grated
    Parmesan
250g short pasta, e.g.
    fusilli or penne

Get the pasta water boiling. The rest of the dish takes very little time.

Melt the butter in a small saucepan and stir in the flour with a wooden spoon. Season well with salt and lots of freshly ground black pepper, and cook gently for a few minutes. Add the chopped shallot and cook for a few minutes more, just to soften slightly. Now add the milk gradually, stirring well to remove any lumps. Simmer for 15 minutes with regualr stirring while you get the pasta cooking. When the sauce is done, stir in half the cheeses. Keep warm on the hob, and reheat if necessary to get it really hot before tossing with the pasta.

Cook the pasta according to the instructions on the packet, but take it out a minute or so before it is fully cooked. Drain well and tip into a small ovenproof dish. Toss with the sauce and sprinkle on the remaining cheeses. Cook at 200°C at the top of the oven, about 5 minutes to get a lightly browned crust; about 10 if you prefer a really crunchy crust.

baking

What excites me most about halogenic baking is that the oven's size and speed make it eminently practical to bake just one or two small things. If you keep a bowl of bread dough covered with clingfilm, in the fridge, you can snip off a little and bake something tasty in a matter of minutes. But that's not where it ends, because the halogen oven can handle just about any shape and size of bread you throw at it, and with some easy modifications they're no trickier than in the big oven. And it isn't just breads: pizza-type recipes and stuffed dishes also work well – ample reasons to keep that bit of dough always at the ready.

This makes twelve pitta breads or two small loaves. Try to use stone-ground, unbleached flour, and I would recommend a combination of white and wholemeal flour. If you want the bread to rise faster, use 1 level tablespoon of yeast.

ready-to-go bread dough

makes 1.1kg dough

425ml water
2 level teaspoons active
   dried yeast
675g strong flour (white
   or a combination of
   white and wholemeal)
1–2 teaspoons salt
vegetable oil

Put the water in a large mixing bowl. You can heat it to a lukewarm temperature of 35–40°C for faster frothing, but cold water works too. Add the yeast and leave it for 5–10 minutes, until it starts to froth up a little. In the meantime, measure out the flour and the salt.

Now add all the salt and the flour a cupful at a time, mixing it in each time. Don't worry about lumps. Keep going until the dough feels too stiff for stirring, then start kneading. Put some flour on your hands and a little more on the top of the dough and turn out onto a clean work surface. Knead by lifting the ball of dough and folding or pushing it down. As you knead, the ball will become more resilient. If it still feels wet and sticky, add a little more flour. Don't be afraid to use all the flour, but don't feel you must if it seems too much.

When the dough feels springy, smooth, firm and elastic, shape it into a neat ball. Pour a little vegetable oil in the mixing bowl and turn the ball in the oil so it is covered completely, then cover tightly with a plate or clingfilm. Leave it about 1–2 hours at room temperature until it has roughly doubled in size. Then punch it down by pressing firmly all over the ball with your fist, and knead the dough again briefly. Now you can let it rise again to double its size (covered) before punching down and forming into your chosen loaf, or – if you are in a hurry – form the loaves straight away.

This dough will keep, tightly covered, in the fridge for 4–5 days.

It took me a few tries to achieve a conventional shaped loaf in the halogen oven, but I got there in the end. Here's the secret: keep the loaf low down in the oven so the top doesn't brown too quickly and then turn it out of the tin to finish baking with the bottom facing up.

an everyday loaf

makes 1 large loaf

vegetable oil
half-quantity bread
   dough (see page 113)
1 free-range egg, beaten
plain flour

Lightly oil a small loaf tin and form the dough into a squat brick-shaped piece that will fit snugly in the bottom. Leave it to rise, covered, until it's high enough to reach three-quarters of the way up the walls of the tin.

Brush the top with egg and sprinkle on some flour. Put on the rack at the lowest point in the oven, put on the extender ring and bake at 200°C for 20 minutes. Lift the tin out carefully and place a clean roasting rack over the top. Invert the tin and see if the loaf slips out. If it needs more time before it slips out, put it back in for another 5 minutes and try again. Then put the loaf back in the oven directly on the rack, with the bottom facing up, and bake for another 10 minutes or so, until the loaf feels hollow when tapped.

variation: onion and cumin loaf

Gently knead the dough with half a small onion, finely chopped, and 1 teaspoon of cumin seeds or powder mixed in. Let it rise, then bake as in the recipe.

This makes a big wide flattish loaf – excellent for slicing thinly, toasting and serving with paté or cheese.

a big round loaf

makes 1 large loaf

vegetable oil
half-quantity bread
  dough (see page 113)

Lightly oil a 25cm dish. Shape the ball of dough to fit in snugly. It will end up being about 5–7.5cm high in the middle. Bake for about 20 minutes at 225°C at the bottom of the oven, turning towards the end of cooking (see page 114) to make sure the base is fully cooked and has taken on a nice colour.

This loaf illustrates perfectly the flexibility you have with baking in the halogen oven. No-one in their right mind would consider turning on a great big conventional oven just to bake a single miniature baguette. But in the halogen oven, the whole operation seems much more approachable.

a small baguette

makes 1 small
baguette

175g bread dough (see
  page 113), a piece
  about the size of
  your fist
plain flour

Shape the dough into a cylinder, tapered at both ends, about 20cm long. Cut a few slashes on the bias and leave to rise for at least 20 minutes (you can leave it for much longer if this suits you). Dust with flour and bake at 200°C at the middle of the oven for 20–25 minutes. Two baguettes can easily be baked at the same time.

I discovered this one by accident. The ring contracts during baking until it forms a solid mass with an attractive pattern on top. And the centre of the ring can be filled with something tasty, which will then get absorbed by the roll. Fun and good. Needless to say, you can omit the spice if you wish, or come up with your own ideas for flavouring.

spicy ring roll

makes 1 bread roll

150g bread dough (see page 113), a piece slightly smaller than a tennis ball
extra virgin olive oil
pinch of spices of your choice, such as cumin seeds, fennel seeds, dill or caraway

Shape the dough into a cylinder, as even in diameter as possible, about 15cm long. Fold the cylinder to connect the ends, overlapping them slightly and pressing down to pinch them together. Lightly oil a baking sheet and place the dough on it. Put a dribble of oil in the centre, followed by a pinch of spices of your choice. Bake at 225°C at the top of the oven for about 10 minutes, until the top is nicely browned. As the roll cooks, you will see the ring contract and form itself into a perfectly shaped ball. Turn over and cook with the bottom up for a couple of minutes more to make sure it is done all the way through.

These fresh-from-the-oven flatbreads make a welcome addition to a weekend lunch, or appetising nibbles to serve with drinks.

crisp flatbreads

makes 2

150g bread dough (see page 113), a piece slightly smaller than a tennis ball
extra virgin olive oil
chopped or dried herbs of your choice
thinly sliced cheese (optional)

Divide the dough into two pieces. Roll out in circles about 20cm in diameter or ovals of comparable size; the dough will be very thin, so handle with extreme care. Put them 2 at a time on a flat ovenproof baking sheet (brushing the sheet first with vegetable oil if it does not have a non-stick coating) and let them rise in a warm place for a minimum of 10 minutes and a maximum of 30. Sprinkle with extra virgin olive oil and some chopped or dried herbs and thinly sliced cheese if you wish. Cook near the top of the oven for about 4–5 minutes at 225°C. The finished breads can be kept at room temperature while you bake more.

You can cook a maximum of three at a time
of these excellent little flatbreads.

pitta breads

makes 3

plain flour
225g bread dough
   (see page 113)

Snip off 2 or 3 pieces of dough weighing about 75g each.
Roll out into circles about 12.5cm in diameter or ovals
of comparable size. Put them on a flat baking sheet
and let them rise for a minimum of 10 minutes and a
maximum of 30. Cook near the top of the oven for about
10 minutes at 225°C. The finished breads can be kept
at room temperature while you bake more.

These can be ready in ten minutes from the
snipping of the dough to serving.

super-quick breadsticks

makes 1

plain flour
25g bread dough
   (see page 113)
coarse salt

Put plenty of flour on your hands and roll out the dough
until it's about 15cm long. You may have to stretch it if
rolling is difficult, but try not to. Sprinkle with coarse salt
and cook at 225°C at the top of the oven until lightly
browned, about 5 minutes. You can cook up to
6 breadsticks at a time.

Italian calzoni, semicircles of pizza dough stuffed with any number of ingredients, are wonderful things. But they can be a little too filling unless you want to make an entire meal out of them. These miniature versions are the solution, great as starters or canapés (halved) or for a lightish weekend lunch.

calzoncini

makes about 20

600g bread dough
    (see page 113)
plain flour
tasty stuff for the
    stuffing (see below)
extra virgin olive oil
1 egg yolk, optional

Snip off a piece of dough about the size of a golf ball. Flour it lightly, then generously flour your work surface and roll the dough out into a roughly circular shape about 15cm in diameter. Leave to rest for 10 minutes, then fill one half of each circle with about 45g of stuffing. Take care to leave a 2.5cm border between the stuffing and the rim of the dough.

Brush the rim of each with water, then fold the dough over the stuffing and pinch all along the edge to form a tight seal. You can keep them as simple semicircles or twist the corners into an intriguing moustache shape. Brush a baking sheet with oil and place the stuffed calzoncini on it as they're done. Leave to rest for at least 10 minutes. You can refrigerate these for longer if that suits your schedule.

Just before baking, brush the tops with oil (or egg yolk for a shinier finish) and dust with flour if you wish. Cook at 250°C/260°C at the middle of the oven until the tops are golden and the calzoncini are nicely puffed up, about 10–15 minutes.

Filling options
These are just five of my top suggestions. The sky's the limit here, however, so use whatever you have on hand. Chopping all the ingredients into small pieces will increase the amount you can stuff into each pouch.
• Shredded raw courgette and garlic with a few drops
  of extra virgin olive oil
• Thinly sliced celery, onion and fresh sage with a little butter
• Mozzarella and sun-dried tomato, all on their own
• Shredded prosciutto or salami, cherry tomatoes,
  and flaked Parmesan
• Caramelised sliced onions and rosemary

This Italian-style dish uses an olive-oil pastry dough inspired by the one I read about in *In Nonna's Kitchen*, by the outstanding American cookery writer Carol Field. Some good news for vegetarians: you can omit the bacon and the torta will still taste great.

spinach and red pepper torta

serves 6–8

For the pastry dough
300g plain flour
100ml extra virgin olive oil
large pinch of salt
100–150ml water

For the filling
350g baby spinach
4 thick slices of bacon or pancetta, cut into cubes or thick lardons
2 roasted red peppers (see page 18), cut into small chunks or thin strips
3 free-range eggs, beaten
good grating of nutmeg
salt and freshly ground black pepper
1 free-range egg, beaten

First make the pastry dough. Put the flour in a bowl and make a well in the centre, then pour in the oil and add a good dose of salt. Mix gradually until the mixture resembles cornmeal (Carol Field's description), then add the water gradually, mixing quickly but thoroughly to get a firm dough. Knead the dough very briefly, then roll it up into a neat ball. Cover in clingfilm and refrigerate for 30 minutes while you make the filling.

Cook the spinach very briefly in a covered saucepan or the microwave; it should be barely cooked, just softened but still retaining the shape of each leaf. Put in a sieve and leave to cool. Then squeeze out as much water as possible by pressing a handful at a time between your palms. Put in a mixing bowl.

Cook the bacon or pancetta in a small frying pan just until it gives up a good amount of its fat and browns slightly. Add to the spinach, leaving behind some of the rendered fat if you prefer. Add the peppers and eggs, grate in the nutmeg, and season well.

Divide the dough in two pieces, making one slightly larger than the other. Roll out the smaller piece to line a fairly deep 20cm pie dish. Lift it into place using the rolling pin and press down around the edges to make sure it fills out the dish. Spoon in the filling, smoothing it flat, then roll out the other piece of dough, lay it on top and crimp the edges to seal. Poke a few holes in it so steam can escape. Brush the top with beaten egg and cook at 200°C at the middle of the oven until the top is golden and the contents piping hot, about 30 minutes.

puddings

The halogen oven will keep the sweet-toothed happy for quite some time. The trick is to keep things fairly simple. Fruit does incredibly well under the lamp, whether presented on its own, as I do with rhubarb and pineapple, or in more elaborate assemblages. Cakes are a bit tricky: the overhead heat makes very deep cakes impractical, though shallower versions cook much as they do in the conventional oven. As cakes are not the halogen oven's strong suit, I have left them out here to concentrate on other things. There are a couple of tempting options for chocoholics, and don't forget: the halogen oven's compact size and energy efficiency lend themselves to eminently justifiable treats for one.

Seriously simple and highly popular in my house. These quantities are per serving, but you can make up to four at a time, so you could present this at a small dinner party. It's also good without the biscuit.

baked bananas with chocolate

serves 1

1 digestive biscuit
1 small banana, thinly sliced on the bias
25–50g good-quality dark chocolate, grated
1 tablespoon brown sugar
cream, to serve (optional)

Crush the biscuit into the base of an oval or round ceramic flat-bottomed dish or a deep ramekin. Put in half the banana, then the chocolate and then the remaining banana. Sprinkle with the sugar and cook at 200°C at the middle of the oven until the sugar is bubbling merrily and the banana is good and hot, about 15–20 minutes. You can dribble on some cream to serve, if you wish.

Some of the rhubarb turns out perfectly soft, while some retains a bit of firmness. Some gets browned and some doesn't. A nice contrast of textures, and all ready to eat within fifteen minutes, including preparation. You can double the recipe, but use a 25–26cm dish.

quick rhubarb compote

serves 2–3

350g young rhubarb, trimmed and cut into 2.5cm lengths
50g brown sugar
2 tablespoons lemon juice
2 tablespoons sweet wine or water
1 slice of fresh ginger, peeled and finely chopped
3–4 knobs of butter
custard or double cream, to serve

Mix all the ingredients except the butter in a heavy, flat-bottomed dish about 15cm in diameter. Stir really well to try and dissolve the sugar. Cook at 250°C/260°C at grilling position for 7–8 minutes, adding the butter and stirring after 5 minutes. Test by poking several pieces with a small, sharp knife. Some will be completely soft, verging on collapse, while the hardest ones should be easy to pierce. If you want everything to be completely soft, just cook for another 2–3 minutes. Serve with custard or double cream.

I greatly prefer dessert apples to cooking apples when I am making this dish: they need less sugar and they keep their shape better. The only other thing you need to make it work is a melon-baller.

cinnamon-baked apples with marmalade

serves 4

4 good apples (I use Braeburn)
4 pinches of ground cinnamon
2 tablespoons orange or lime marmalade
2 tablespoons brown sugar
8 small knobs of butter
double cream, to serve

Use your melon-baller to cut gradually through the stem-end of each apple and remove the core. Scoop out the core until you're within about 1cm of the base, taking care not to cut all the way through.

Put the apples in a flat-bottomed dish. Drop a pinch of cinnamon in each hollowed-out core. Divide the marmalade equally between the apples, spooning a small dollop into each. Then do the same with the brown sugar. Finally top the sugar with a knob of butter.

Cook at 200°C at the bottom of the oven until the apples are soft but not disintegrating, about 30–35 minutes. Towards the end of cooking, put another knob of butter in each apple for extra richness. Serve hot, with double cream.

Many of the recipes that cookery writers dream up are inspired by other recipes. This one, however, was inspired by the halogen oven itself, because of its ability to grill intensely and roast at the same time. The bottom of the pineapple is just warmed through, while the top is something like pineapple brûlée. It is really splendid and, apart from the careful slicing of the fruit, very easy.

cinnamon and rum pineapple

serves 4-6

1 smallish pineapple, about 12.5cm long, weighing 1kg
2 tablespoons good-quality dark rum (I use a 5- or 7-year-old Añejo)
1 teaspoon ground cinnamon
90ml golden or brown sugar
cream, to serve (optional)

Top and tail the pineapple, then cut in half lengthwise. Using a very sharp paring knife or short-bladed chef's knife, make parallel cuts on the bias through the flesh at 2.5cm intervals, taking the tip of the knife almost to the skin. Try to cut to within about 1cm of the skin, but be careful not to pierce it. Now, if you wish, you can make another set of cuts to form a criss-cross pattern.

Mix the rum and cinnamon well, then pour the mixture over the two pineapple halves and leave to let the liquid seep into the fruit for a couple of minutes.

Sprinkle the sugar over the pineapple halves as evenly as possible. Cook at 250°C/260°C at the middle of the oven until the sugar bubbles and then crisps up, about 10–15 minutes.

To serve, put the pineapple halves on a chopping board and cut thick slices. You can serve this with cream if you wish, but it's simply ambrosial all on its own.

This is a diminutive version of the classic Eve's Pudding.
I've presented it in this size to illustrate how the halogen oven
makes it worthwhile to cook something indulgent, such as a
baked pudding, even for just two people. To make the larger
version, simply double the quantities and use a larger (but not
too much deeper) dish.

little eve's pudding

serves 2

For the filling
2–3 dessert apples
(Granny Smith and
Braeburn are good),
weighing about
350g, cored, peeled and
cut into small dice
2 tablespoons lemon juice
1 tablespoon caster sugar
generous knob of butter

For the sponge
50g butter
50g caster sugar
1 free-range egg, beaten
50g self-raising flour
1 tablespoon boiling
water
double cream or custard,
to serve

Mix the apples, lemon juice and sugar with a few drops of water in a baking dish of about 28 x 20cm. Dot with the butter and cook at 200°C at the middle of the oven, stirring two or three times, until the apples are lightly coloured and nearly cooked, 10–15 minutes.

In the meantime, make the sponge. Cream the butter and sugar until the mixture is pale, then quickly stir in the egg. Now fold in the flour a spoonful at a time. Work quickly and don't overmix so you keep the mixture as fluffy as possible. If you see bits of flour that haven't been absorbed, don't worry: they'll disappear in cooking.

Plop the dough on the fruit a tablespoon at a time; the fruit does not need to be completely covered. Cook at 175°C at the bottom of the oven until the surface is nicely browned and the topping fully cooked, about 40 minutes. The pudding is finished when a knife or skewer stuck into the dish comes out hot and clean. Leave to cool for a few minutes, then serve with double cream or custard.

Clafoutis is more usually made with cherries, but I love the caramelised look (and flavour) when pears are pre-cooked in the halogen oven. You could also make this dish with apples.

pear clafoutis

serves 4

4 small pears, peeled, cored and quartered lengthwise
125g caster sugar
½ teaspoon ground cinnamon
50g butter, cut into small pieces
1 heaped tablespoon flour
4 free-range eggs
60ml single cream (or milk)
icing sugar, to dust (optional)

Take out a heavy ovenproof dish that will hold the fruit fairly snugly in a single layer. Something round, with a diameter of 25cm and a depth of 5cm, would be just right. Put the pears in the dish and toss well with 100g of the sugar and the cinnamon. Dot the small pieces of butter around the fruit. Cook in the middle of the oven at 250°C/260°C until the pears are well softened, about 10 minutes, tossing a few times. If the butter is showing signs of getting too brown, turn the heat down to 200°C. (This recipe may be prepared in advance up to this point and left to cool.)

While the pears are cooking, whisk the rest of the ingredients (including the remaining 25g of sugar) until everything is well blended.

Pour the batter ointo the dish taking care to pour between the pieces of fruit. Continue cooking at 250°C/260°C until the batter puffs up nicely, takes on a bit of colour and crisps up a slightly. This can take as little as 5 minutes if the batter was poured in while the pears were hot, or up to 10 if the whole thing started off at room temperature. Leave for at least 5 minutes before dusting with icing sugar (if you wish) and serving.

You could also make this classic pudding with pears and, if you like it, add some rhubarb to the mixture. If rhubarb goes in, however, you'll need to add more sugar to the fruit.

apple crumble

serves 4–6

900g dessert apples
   (3–6, depending on
   size), peeled, cored,
   and cut into chunks
   about 2.5cm square
25g caster sugar
½ teaspoon ground
   cinnamon
juice of ½ lemon

For the crumble
100g butter
125g flour, preferably a
   combination of white
   and wholemeal
40g caster sugar
a scraping of nutmeg

Toss the fruit, sugar, cinnamon and lemon juice in an ovenproof dish about 12.5cm deep and 20cm in diameter. Cook at 200°C at the middle of the oven for 15 minutes or so. Stir a few times during cooking until the apples are steaming and the sugar has dissolved. Take the dish out of the oven.

While the fruit is cooking, mix all the crumble ingredients together. Take the dish out of the oven and spread the crumble mixture over the fruit as evenly as possible and continue cooking until the topping is crisp and the apples are soft. This should not take more than 30 minutes and may take as little as 25.

Here you can use your favourite pudding wine in the recipe and then drink the remainder of the bottle as you enjoy the dish. A piece of shortbread is the crowning indulgence.

pears with cinnamon, sweet wine and chocolate

serves 4

4 ripe pears, peeled, cored and halved lengthwise
fragment of cinnamon stick
60ml sweet white wine
60ml caster sugar
50g good-quality dark chocolate
75ml single cream

Take out a heavy ovenproof dish that will hold the fruit fairly snugly in a single layer. Something round, with a diameter of 25cm and a depth of 5cm, would do the trick perfectly. Put the pears and cinnamon stick in the dish, then pour the wine over the fruit and dust with the sugar. Cook in the middle of the oven at 250°C/260°C until the pears are fully cooked, about 15 minutes. Spoon the liquid over them a few times during cooking. If the liquids are evaporating, add a couple of splashes of water.

Remove the pears to serving dishes. Put the chocolate and cream in the cooking dish and place in the oven just long enough to melt the chocolate, about 1–2 minutes. Whisk the sauce to blend well, then pour over the pears and serve immediately. Shortbread would make a good accompaniment.

This dish is ready to eat in barely forty minutes – and that includes ten minutes of cooling time for the finished tart. You can omit the glaze if you're in a hurry: it makes the tart look beautiful, but it isn't strictly necessary.

apple tart

serves 4

200g shortcrust pastry (homemade or ready-made)
100ml apricot jam (optional)
2 good dessert apples (e.g. Granny Smith), peeled, cored and cut into thin wedges
½ teaspoon ground cinnamon
50ml caster sugar
juice of ½ lemon

Roll out the pastry to fit a 20cm pie tin and put it in neatly. Refrigerate for 30 minutes so that it can relax.

In the meantime, make an apricot glaze if you've decided you'd like to glaze the tart. Heat the jam in a small saucepan or the microwave until it is just hot. Push through a fine sieve into a small bowl, trying to squeeze out every bit of syrupy goo. Set aside.

Prick the bottom of the pastry with a fork, line with aluminium foil and put in baking beans to fill. Bake blind in the middle of the oven at 200°C for 10 minutes, then remove beans and bake for another 4–5 minutes, until moderately crisp. Leave to cool slightly for 5–10 minutes before using.

While the crust is cooling, toss the apples with the cinnamon, sugar and lemon juice. Arrange the apple wedges neatly in the tin. Bake in the middle of the oven at 200°C for 20–25 minutes, until the apples are lightly browned and very soft. If you're using the glaze, brush it over the top (this may be easier if you heat it up a little) and leave to cool for at least 10 minutes before serving.

This recipe, adapted from one by Gary Rhodes, calls for dariole moulds with a capacity of 175ml. These are widely available at good cookware shops and are not at all expensive.

hot chocolate fondants

serves 6

150g well-softened butter,
    plus extra for buttering
cocoa powder, for dusting
150g dark chocolate,
    coarsely chopped
3 free-range eggs plus
    3 egg yolks
75ml caster sugar
3 tablespoons plain flour

Butter 6 dariole moulds and dust with cocoa powder. Melt the rest of the butter and chocolate in a large bowl over a saucepan of barely simmering water. Keep the chocolate warm once it has fully melted. Use an electric whisk to cream the eggs, egg yolks and sugar until the mixture is pale and thick, but so airy it has a consistency something like lightly whipped cream. Pour this mixture into the melted chocolate, sift the flour over the top, and fold the flour and egg mixture into the chocolate quickly, gently and thoroughly. Spoon into the moulds, smooth out the tops and cook straightaway or leave in the fridge until they are needed.

Put the moulds on the rack at the bottom of the oven, spacing them well apart. Bake at 200°C and keep a close eye on them. At about 8 minutes they will have risen in a mound shape to a height about 1cm above the rim. Take them out at exactly that point. Leave to rest for a minute before turning them out. They should be cake-like on the outside with a molten, gooey core.

The diminutive size of the halogen oven makes it a difficult appliance for cooking more than one dish at a time. I've tried it, and the logistics just don't work out very well. But if you plan your meal right, with at least one dish served at room temperature and/or one pudding that can be cooked while you're eating, you can manage a whole meal. And because the oven cooks so fast, you can have a complete meal on the table in as little as 20 minutes. Here are a few suggestions.

menu suggestions

a quick midweek dinner

One-Sided salmon (page 56)
Roast New Potatoes with Rosemary and Sage (page 102)
Blackened French Beans (page 28)

Cook the beans first for serving at room temperature. Do the potatoes next, then finally blast away at the salmon.

a light springtime lunch

Asparagus and Onion Frittata (page 39)
Fast Fresh Fennel (page 17)
Quick Rhubarb Compote (page 126)

All of these can be served at room temperature so the work order is up to you, but I would do the rhubarb first, followed by the frittata and then (giving the oven a quick wipe) the fennel.

a special dinner for two

Fish and Bacon Kebabs (page 54)
Rolled Steak with Duxelles (page 95)
Hot Chocolate Fondants (page 138)

Cook the kebabs and then, while you're eating, the beef. When you're nearly done with the main course, give the oven a quick wipe and cook the fondants.

dinner for six

Roast Chicken and Some Vegetables (page 64)
Warm Coleslaw (page 27)
Patatas Gordas (page 104)
Apple Crumble (page 134)

Do the coleslaw first (it tastes great at room temperature), then the chicken. Cook the spuds while the chicken is resting – you can reduce the chicken juices in a pot on the hob if you wish – and put the crumble in while you're eating the main course.

a vegetarian feast

Stuffed Aubergines (page 30)
Roasted Beetroot (page 28)
Roasted Mushrooms (page 35)
Spanish Tortilla (page 39)
Cinnamon and Rum Pineapple (page 128)

All of these can be served at room temperature so the work order is up to you, but I would do the beetroot and mushrooms first, followed by the tortilla and then the aubergines. The pineapple can cook while you're eating everything else.

meat and potatoes

Free-form Meatloaf (page 96) *or* Lightning-quick Lamb Joint
  (page 87) *or* Rib of Beef (page 91)
Potato Wedges (page 103)
Roasted Cherry Tomatoes (page 24)
Cinnamon-baked Apples with Marmalade (page 127)

Do the tomatoes first, then the meat; leave the meat to rest while you cook the potatoes, and bake the apples while you're eating.

index

acknowledgements

My first thanks go to all at Kyle Cathie Publishing, and especially to Kyle Cathie herself, whose suggestion that I investigate halogen ovens changed my cooking life forever. Jenny Wheatley, my editor, handled my copy and my slipping deadlines with her usual care, skill and tact. Constance Novis copy-edited with an acute eye. Will Heap, Jane Lawrie and Sue Rowlands made the photographs look ravishing. Mark Latter designed the book with grace and clarity.

My agent, Anna Power of Johnson & Alcock, remains my champion and my truest believer.

Thanks also to the cookery writers whose ideas I adapted for use in the halogen oven. If my adaptations fall short, this does not reflect on the models.

My family, especially my wife Emma Dally and my youngest daughter, Ruth, put up with endless grief during the months I tested recipes – not all of them successful. I thank them – and my other daughters, Rebecca and Alice – for their forbearance and helpful advice.

Finally I thank my brother Henry, of Brooklyn, New York. Henry let me test recipes in his home kitchen, contributed a few of his own, and gave an abundance of useful advice.